A WORDSWORTH HANDBOOK

20TH-CENTURY STEAM

Wordsworth Editions

First published in England 1994 by
Wordsworth Editions Ltd
Cumberland House
Crib Street
Ware
Hertfordshire SG12 9ET

ISBN 1–85326–816–X

Previous page: **the ultimate steam locomotive, a Union
Pacific Big Boy, doing what it does best**

Opposite: **a Royal Scot Class 4–6–0 locomotive, first built
for LMS in 1927**

Designed and produced by Superlaunch Ltd
P O Box 207, Abingdon, Oxfordshire OX13 6TA, England
Text conversion and pagination by
August Filmsetting, St Helens, England
Colour separation by Seagull Reproductions Ltd, London
Printed and bound in the Czech Republic by Svoboda

CONTENTS

EUROPE
Austria   4
Belgium   7
Czechoslovakia   8
France   9
Germany   21
Great Britain   30
Italy   45
Spain   47
Switzerland   48
Wagon-Lits and Luxury Travel   50
UNITED STATES OF
AMERICA   55
CANADA   73
SOUTH AMERICA   76
INDIA AND THE PACIFIC   77
AFRICA   93
PICTURE GALLERY   87
WHEEL NOTATION   90
HOW IT WORKS   92
INDEX   94
ACKNOWLEDGMENTS   96

EUROPE

Austria

A country that has more than its fair share of mountains, Austria, Switzerland's eastern neighbour, was the centre of a Balkan empire before the First World War reshaped Europe. Both private and state railways were built in the nineteenth century, always with strategic requirements dictating the location of many of the long-distance routes that connected with the railways of neighbouring countries.

Many of the services involved the negotiation of steep, sharply curving lines, and Karl Gölsdorf's locomotives, which predominated on Austrian railways at the turn of the century, were based on the compound system.

Imperial and Royal Austrian State Railways' (KKStB's) traction chief from 1891, Gölsdorf had miraculously contrived a wide-firebox, 210.2cm (6ft 10.75in) driving-wheel express engine which did not flout the civil engineers' rules, by inverting the Pacific layout into a 2-6-4.

Gölsdorf's own refinement of the compound method was the introduction of an arrangement of steam inlets that

Class 310 2-6-4

Railway: Imperial and Royal State Railway (KKStB)
Date: 1908
Length overall: 21.318m (69ft 11in)
Total weight: 146,000kg (322,000lb)
Cylinders: high-pressure, two 390 × 720mm (15.4 × 28.3in); low-pressure, two 620 × 720mm (24.4 × 28.3in)
Driving wheels: 21m (7ft 10.7in)
Axle load: 14,600kg (32,200lb)
Fuel: 8,500kg (19,000lb)
Grate area: 4.6m² (49.7sq ft)
Water: 21m³ (4,620 Imp gal/5,550 US gal)
Heating surface: 193m² (2,077sq ft)
Superheater: 43m² (463sq ft)
Steam pressure: 15kg/cm² (213psi)
Adhesive weight: 44,000kg (98,000lb)
History: Austria ran 43 of these super lightweight expresses until 1957. Designed by Karl Gölsdorf, the four-cylinder locos were ideally suited fully to utilise the poor quality coal, and yet produce so much power. A further 10 engines were built and exported to Prussia (seven) and Poland (three).

A Class 210, the two-cylinder forerunner of the Class 310

passed steam directly to the low-pressure cylinders to start or for low-pressure working, but switching automatically to compound operation as the cut-off of the steam was shortened.

Gölsdorf was also a great inventor in the matter of wheel arrangements, producing the first 2-6-2 engines in Europe and the first 2-6-4 and 2-12-0 types to appear anywhere, specialising in models with large numbers of driving wheels with a wheelbase flexible enough for the sharp curves. One of the most popular types for the heavy work in the conditions encountered on the difficult Austrian lines was the 4-8-0, and the class

33 locomotives produced after Gölsdorf's death were able to handle curves of less than 121.9m (400ft) radius.

By the outbreak of the First World War, however, railways operating in a mountainous environment like those in Austria and Spain appreciated that the bulk of their express passenger traffic was best served by the greater adhesion weight of an eight-coupled engine, of which the 175.3cm (5ft 9in) driving wheel 4-8-0 conceived by the Austrian Südbahn for its Semmering Pass main line in 1914 was a pre-eminent example.

The railway system most drastically reformed by the Allied Powers was without question the Austrian. The Versailles Treaty's restructuring of the European map after the First World War sheared away 72% of the pre-war Austrian rail mileage and also proportionate locomotives and rolling stock.

In 1920 there were only ten express trains daily into and out of Vienna's seven terminals. At the start of the 1920s, it was recognised that the pillage of Austrian equipment had been overdone and an equitable number of locomotives and vehicles were returned. The need was so acute that few were given more than first-aid treatment before being put back into Austrian traffic, while the precarious state of the economy, with its inflation rate little less than sky high, deferred any new construction until 1923.

The condition of the Austrian railway system was to be aggravated further by the territorial adjustments that followed the Second World War, the effects of which lingered into the 1980s.

Under the Austro-Hungarian Empire, the railway network had developed along a northeast to south axis, with Vienna at the centre; now the focus was primarily east to west, a flow to which the railway facilities of Vienna itself were particularly ill-suited. Main lines such as the Arlberg, built as single track, would now be loaded with traffic flows far heavier than had been envisaged before the war; in contrast, other once-vital arterial routes had become irremediably unviable not only by truncation but because they had been severed from their main sources of industrial freight.

Austrian State Railway was run as a government department, which was no sort of *régime* to grapple effectively with the system's grievous post-war problems. Prodded by the Allies, Austria had reconstituted its railway as a separate, commercially-based undertaking in October 1923, but one with considerable statutory obligations. Entitled the Austrian Federal Railway (ÖBB), it took control officially at the start of 1924.

Among all the other Versailles Treaty deprivations, Austria had been cut off from its own previously indigenous sources of good-quality steam coal. That, and the belief that another form of traction would enlarge single-track operating capacity sufficiently to avoid the dauntingly expensive and difficult double-tracking of its mountain pass routes, decided ÖBB to pursue electrification and by 1935 it had converted four main lines.

Belgium

The assertive role of so many nineteenth-century governments in railway network development had actually culminated in nationalisation, as in Italy, or else it had the stage well set for a final act of unification. In some countries, such as Sweden and Belgium, a State railway already in being was progressively taking over private companies: in Belgium that process reached the point of nationalisation in 1926.

In the spring of 1939, Belgian National Railways (SNCB) first installed a twice-daily service of three-car trains over its easily-graded, well-aligned route between Bruxelles and Oostende which was scheduled over the 92.4km (57.4 miles) from the Belgian capital to Bruges at an average of 120.5km/h (74.9mph) start to stop. For its traction, the SNCB created a sextet of 209.6cm (6ft 10.5in) 4-4-2s, each looking like some malformed flying fish with its large smoke-deflector plates set apart from a bulbous streamlined casing that completely concealed its chimneys. One of these Atlantics was logged at a smart 165km/h (102.5mph) on the service's maximum permitted load of five cars. It allowed the Belgians a brief tenure of the title of operators of the Continent's fastest daily train.

A Belgian streamlined Class 12 4-4-2 at Tournai in June 1959

Czechoslovakia

Class 498.1 4-8-2

Czechoslovakia was a country that after the First World War favoured the eight-coupled locomotive as a maid of all work. It built a family of three-cylinder simple and compound 182.9cm (6ft) wheel 4-8-2s from 1934 onwards, and also bred a two-cylinder simple version with slightly smaller wheels in 1948. This and the concluding three cylinder 1954 versions of the Czech 4-8-2s, all of which had Kylchap double exhausts, mechanical stokers and various other refinements derived eclectically from recent French, German and American practice, ranked amongst the most sophisticated products of European steam's final era.

Railway: Czechoslovakia State Railways (ČSD)
Date: 1954
Length overall: 25.59m (83ft 11.5in)
Total weight: 194,000kg (428,500lb)
Cylinders: three 500 × 680mm (19.75 × 26.75in)
Driving wheels: 1.83m (6ft)
Axle load: 16,800-18,500kg (37,000-41,000lb)
Fuel: 15,000kg (33,000lb)
Grate area: 4.9m² (52sq ft)
Water: 35m³ (7,700 Imp gal/9,200 US gal)
Superheater: 74m² (797sq ft)

Czechoslovakia no longer runs steam locomotives but one Class 498.1 4-8-2 has been preserved

France

In the twentieth century's first quarter, French locomotive technology was dominated by the de Glehn system of four-cylinder compounding. He had evolved and applied the system to Nord Railway engines, in conjunction with that company's locomotive chief, de Bousquet. The Nord's compound Atlantic of 1901 was Europe's stellar express passenger performer of the period, exciting attention outside as well as within Europe by its proclivity for speed, combined with striking up-grade power in relation to its size, which the class displayed on the prestigious Paris to Calais boat trains.

Right up to 1939 these engines, by then fitted with more capacious tenders and treated to such latter-day efficiency aids as a multiple-jet blastpipe and chimney, were still deployed on tightly-timed, limited-load Paris-Bruxelles luxury trains like the *Oiseau Bleu* Pullman and the 'Nord Express'. They were quite capable, too, of keeping the 406 tonne (400 ton) Paris-Calais boat trains rolling on level track at 121km/h (75mph), the speed ceiling imposed on all French railways since the mid-

nineteenth century and not relaxed until 1937, when the decidedly modest increase to 130km/h (81mph) was granted over just a few well-aligned stretches of main line. This limitation predisposed French express passenger locomotive designers to concentrate on power output, since the faster journey times demanded were attainable only to the extent that the maximum permissible speed could be maintained or approached on the flat and uphill. That specification was becoming harder to fulfil, because train weights were advancing as European railways recognised that even the ordinary traveller must now be treated to roomier, better furnished coaching stock.

The prowess of the Nord Atlantics persuaded several European railways to persist with the 4-4-2 as their prime express passenger type, rather than risk a confrontation with their civil engineers over the heavy impact on track and nineteenth-century bridges of recent bigger-boilered six-coupled designs. Others, for example in Britain, France and Prussian Germany had fully accepted the 4-6-0 by the outbreak of the First World War, and in France and Germany the pioneer European 4-6-2s had

9

already taken to the tracks by 1907.

Development of the Pacific type in France reflected the contrast between British and Continental tradition in the shaping of motive power policy. Except for on the Paris-Lyons-Méditerranée (PLM), which had stuck to its own system of compounding, each railway's Pacific design up to the outbreak of the First World War, starting with the first Pacific obtained by the Paris-Orléans Railway in 1907, was a four-cylinder compound that was derived fundamentally from de Glehn's exceptional Atlantic. The Nord was nearly a further exception. Until 1912 it was content with a successful, but relatively small-wheeled 4-6-0 which de Bousquet was compel-

A Class 4500 4-6-2 four-cylinder de Glehn compound locomotive of the Paris-Orléans Railway, first built in 1907

led to favour to satisfy the Nord civil engineers' insistence that their track would not tolerate a heavier axle-load than 16.2 tonnes (15.94 tons). By that date British engineers were able to design for 20.32 tonnes (20 tons).

However, these engines, to be classified 230D by the nationalised French Railways, proved remarkably effective express passenger hauliers because de Bousquet had most prudently enlarged their steam passages to accelerate the flow of steam and match the higher piston speeds resulting from driving wheel diameter reduction. When the Nord's civil engineers took track strengthening in hand, de Bousquet prepared a 4-6-4 design and put two proto-types into production, but he died before their completion. The pair were later completed but disenchanted his succes-sors, who were drafting their own Pacific when war put a stop to the Nord's track recon-struction.

During the war the French Government, eyeing the fast-approaching date when the operating concessions granted to the railway companies in the previous century would lapse, thought to set the stage for the full-scale nationalisation it craved by forcing the pace on motive standardisation. A highly proficient new four-cylinder compound 4-6-2 just introduced on the État Railway looked to be just the right tool for the start of the exercise and Government orders for no fewer than 400 of them were placed in the final years of the War (45 were erected by a British firm, the North British Locomotive Company). However, the Nord, along with the PLM and Paris-Orléans, fended off a permanent allocation of État Pacifics and its traction chief Collin pur-sued his own design, which was to materialise as undoubtedly the highest ranking European express engine of the 1920s.

The Nord 'Super-Pacifics', as the French railwaymen justifi-ably tagged them, emerged in an initial batch of 40 in 1923-24, when the railway's main lines were at last fit for an axle load of 18.2 tonnes (17.91 tons). No design of the period was more scientifically considered in its every detail. They had the benefit of bigger cylinders and 10% more adhesion weight than preceding French Pacifics, plus a 102kg (225lb) pressure boiler.

Most importantly, they had the benefit of abnormally large steam passages which had proved a crucial factor in the Nord 4-6-0's efficiency, enabling these Super-Pacifics to spear-head a rapid advance in the average speed of French expresses. In the mid-1920s the 12.9km (8 miles) at 1 in 200 from Wood Green to Potters Bar of the LNER exit from Kings Cross would reduce a Gresley Pacific towing 508 tonnes (500 tons) to 64km/h (40mph) at best by the summit; but on a slope of identical length beginning 14.5km (9 miles) out of Paris' Gare du Nord, a Collin Super, when stopped by signals at the bank's foot, was timed to accelerate a 559 tonne (550 ton) Calais boat train from rest to 92km/h (57mph) within the first 8.1km (5 miles) of the climb: proof enough of the French machine's supremacy. One English observer after another riding the Calais boat trains was dumbfounded by the Supers' ability to hold a steady pace up long slopes with loads of this magnitude, sometimes even accelerating before they reached the crown of the hill.

In 1925 both the Est and PLM Railways rolled out big-wheel 4-8-2s; and three years later, inverting the layout to accommodate the roomy firebox essential for effective combustion of the country's execrable coal, the Austrians unveiled a 2-8-4 with 194.3cm (6ft 4.5in) driving wheels. Was the Pacific an ephemeral phase of development? Could the inexorable commercial pressure for more speed with trains growing progressively heavier because of public demand for better-quality accommodation be met only by bigger boilers and the chassis to go with them? On both counts the answer was no.

That the demands were satisfied more economically on many railways was in large measure a tribute to the genius of France's André Chapelon. In the mid-1920s, he was a research engineer with the Paris-Orléans Railway, and Chapelon was asked to investigate why his company's new Pacifics were bafflingly incapable of

bettering the work of the 4-4-2s they succeeded. Deciding that the problem was deep seated, Chapelon soon embarked on a methodical re-examination of the processes of converting heat into locomotive energy.

From this, with the support of practical dynamometer car tests of existing locomotives on the road, he concluded that contemporary locomotive design was heading up a blind alley. The free running at speed and higher power expected from bigger and bigger locomotives was not forthcoming because orthodox design practice was incapable of optimising the boiler's potential. Only when the engines were on loose rein was full value obtained from the coal and water consumed. As soon as they were pushed for extra speed they disappointed, because the traditional layout of steam passages choked on the boiler's increased output and dissipated a good deal of the steam's power before it reached the piston heads. Some of Chapelon's predecessors, in particular Churchwood of Britain's GWR, had grasped the importance of improving steam circulation; but none had previously undertaken such a scientific study of the question or devised such a detailed pro-

A Class 231C 4-6-2 of PLM, first introduced in 1912; they saw service until the late 1960s

Class 231C 4-6-2

Railway: Paris, Lyons and Mediterranean Railway (PLM)
Length overall: 20m (65ft 7in)
Total weight: 145,500kg (320,500lb)
Cylinders: high-pressure, two 440 × 650mm (17.3 × 25.6in); low-pressure, two 650 × 650 (25.6 × 25.6in)
Driving wheels: 2m (6ft 6.7in)
Axle load: 18,500kg (40,500lb)
Fuel: 5,000kg (11,000lb)
Grate area: 4.3m² (45.7sq ft)
Water: 28m³ (6,160 Imp gal/7,400 US gal)

gramme of re-design as a solution.

Thus the Chapelon theory, broadly speaking, propounded two interdependent lines of action. To maximise the steam output for a given coal and water consumption, a higher degree of superheating must be applied and more efficient draughting be contrived. The latter was secured by fitting a double instead of a single blastpipe and chimney, a concept in which Chapelon refined the work of a Finnish engineer named Kylala – hence the 'Kylchap' name by which the Chapelon system came subsequently to be known. Alongside these changes in the process of

13

steam production Chapelon prescribed a smoothing and doubling of the size of the steam passages throughout, coupled with an increase of piston valve size and travel. Further research convinced the French that the new layout was best complemented by the poppet valves, cam-operated by Walschaert's gear that was otherwise conventional, but some railways did not regard this as an essential concomitant of Chapelon practice. A 50% uplift in performance and striking improvement in fuel economy were the instant results from a prototype rebuilding of one of the previously sluggish P-O Pacifics to the Chapelon specification. Thereafter Chapelon theory became integral, not only to all French steam locomotive practice but to that of many other countries' engineers too.

No more eight-coupled express passenger designs were taken to mass production in Europe until 1934.

Chapelon had evolved his theory primarily for the compound expansion system which predominated in the French railways' express passenger locomotive studs, but in most respects it was just as valid for simple expansion designs. Considering the prowess of later Chapelon-inspired compounds in France, both rebuilds of existing types and of the brand new classes, it is nevertheless surprising the engineers in other countries could not be persuaded to reassess compound propulsion in their adaptations of the rest of Chapelon's principles.

It is true that until 1934 European interest in eight-coupled express passenger design was confined to the French PLM's production of its one-off class 241C 4-8-2 in 1930. The epic performance of some essentially mixed traffic 4-8-0s, the driving wheels of which were only 179.1cm (5ft 10.5in) in diameter, which were reconstructed by Chapelon in 1932-4 from a dozen P-O Pacifics, must not be overlooked, however. These engines were rebuilds in name, although by the time all Chapelon's precepts had been embodied in the redraft most of the original 4-6-2 components must have been discarded.

Of the many striking demonstrations of uphill power obtained from these compound 4-8-0s, in which an extra axle added the benefit of greater adhesion weight to those of Chapelon's own thermodynamic practice, the most impressive was probably that staged with a 645.22 tonne (635

The single-class 241C

ton) train between Calais and Paris in 1935. For this trial the statutory French 121km/h (75mph) speed limit of the period was waived, though one wonders who had expected a machine with such moderately-sized driving wheels to take much advantage of the licence.

Almost at once, though, after lifting the 645.22 tonnes (635 tons) up the 10.9km (6.75 mile), 1.25% (1 in 125) Caffiers bank out of Calais at a minimum of 82km/h (51mph), this 4-8-0 touched 137km/h (85mph) on the descent to Boulogne. Later in the trip the engine actually accelerated its train from 122 to

almost 129km/h (76-80mph) on the long 1.33% (1 in 133) ascent beyond Amiens, then sprinted up to 143km/h (89mph) on a favourable slope to Creil, held at 109–114km/h (68–71mph) all the way up the ensuing 0.5% (1 in 200) Survilliers bank and hit 147km/h (91mph) on the 0.5% (1 in 200) downhill to the Paris suburbs. Not the least spectacular of Chapelon's 4-8-0's feats that day was its maintenance of a 128.3km/h (79.7mph) average throughout 75km (46.6 miles) of level track beyond Étaples, an achievement which similarly-dimensioned Pacifics with notably larger driving wheels never bettered. In 1940 the SNCF transformed 25 more P-O Pacifics in the same fashion,

Previous pages, main picture:
Class 141R No 420 in April 1982;
above left *a 141R at Calais*
Maritime above right *141R.86*
storms out of Boulogne with the
15.31 for Paris in August 1967

but with the additional refinement of mechanical stokers:
these were the SNCF's Class
240P.

The French Nord and PLM
Railways amassed large fleets
of mixed traffic 2-8-2s in the
1930s. After the war the SNCF
modernised them, but simultaneously accumulated an even
bigger stud of two of its own
brands, the four-cylinder com-
pounded Class 141P and the
two-cylinder simple Class 141R.
Over 1,300 141Rs, a 165.1cm (5ft
5in) wheeled type, had been
acquired from US and Canadian
builders. Many of these arrived
pre-equipped with mechanical
stokers, but when coal was at a
premium in the immediate
post-war years the SNCF converted a considerable number
to burn oil.

In 1935 the PLM streamlined
two existing 4-4-2s of its 221A
class and matched them with a
pair of specially built and aero-
dynamically-shaped four-car
train-sets. After trials in which
speeds verging on 161km/h
(100mph) were logged, the two
trainsets were installed in

public Paris-Lyons service in
July 1935. Their five-hour time
allowance for the 512.1km
(318.2-mile) journey in each
direction was less adventurous,
however, than the schedules set
for the streamliner which the
LNER was to première just over
two months later. And the
French trains were unveiled
with nothing like the *éclat* of
the LNER's record-breaking
streamliner launch.

Until the formation of the
unified SNCF in 1938, various
French railways' traction
chiefs were directing their
energies mainly to the rebuilding of their pre-existing
front-rank steam power to the
Chapelon formula, some only
partially, but some to the last
detail. These locomotives were
4-6-2s and 4-8-2s so far as the
express passenger traction was
concerned, and in every case
the performance was mat-
erially improved. Although the
French compounds were still
indisputably more thrifty with
coal than were their simple
expansion counterparts elsewhere, however, the rising cost
of keeping their intricate
mechanisms in good order was
furrowing a few brows. Under
question, too, was the machin-
ery's durability in the face of
ever more oppressive commercial demands, which by the late

1930s were extending to the operation of 1,016 tonne (1,000 ton) freights at mean speeds of 81km/h (50mph) as well as 762 tonne (750 ton) passenger *rapides* at averages in excess of 97km/h (60mph), yet within a 121km/h (75mph) ceiling.

After the Second World War when France was liberated, only 17,992km (11,180 miles) of the full 42,486km (26,400 route miles) operated in 1939 were usable, and this attenuated system was effectively cut in two by the destruction of all bridges over the Loire river below Roanne. On the SNCF as a whole, 2,603 bridges and viaducts had been destroyed, along with a third of all buildings. Of the 17,058 steam locomotives with which the SNCF entered the war, only 10,500 could be unearthed at the Liberation and 7,500 of them were unsuitable. Half the pre-war wagon stock had disappeared; one quarter of what was left was a write-off; and only 7,800 of the 16,900 passenger coaches left in France were runners, whereas the pre-war fleet of such vehicles had totalled 37,700.

Both in France and in the Low Countries, rehabilitation of the railway system was accorded high priority as a key to the revival of economic life. With the crucial assistance of Marshall Aid dollars from the USA, recovery was extraordinarily rapid. As early as May 1946, the SNCF had 40,233km (25,000 route-miles), 95%, of its system back in use. By July 1948, following deliveries of massive orders for locomotives (principally the 1,323 Class 141R 2-8-2s referred to earlier), and rolling stock, placed mostly in the US and Canada, the SNCF had some 12,500 steam locos, 1,200 electric locomotives, 17,300 passenger cars and also 320,000 freight wagons, all fully operational. In 1947, astonishingly, it was able to move 20.5% more passengers and 6.2% more freight tonnage than it had in 1938, over substantially longer distances on average in both categories.

On the very eve of war, some French railway officers had already been urging trunk route electrification as the only economical course; the plans for the first scheme, from Paris to Lyons, were in fact formulated during the country's German occupation. Although Chapelon's alternative of a new range of super-powered, six-cylinder compounds had been rejected (except for building a prototype 2-12-0 freight engine in 1946, that amply fulfilled Chapelon's power prospectus but daunting in its fearsome

mechanical complexity), and though post-war procurement had been dominated by the importation of the 1,323 classically simple two-cylinder 141R 2-8-2s, the SNCF did not entirely eschew new high-power steam passenger engine construction. Between 1940 and 1949 the Nord Region was handed a family of eight elegantly streamlined 4-6-4s, three of them three-cylinder simple expansion (Class 232R) and five four-cylinder compound (Class 232S and the unique Class 232U). The solitary No 232U1, though not delivered until 1949, was arguably the most sophisticated steam locomotive ever to be constructed in Europe, embodying a wealth of power-operated devices to simplify the driver's mastery of its management on the road, not to

The solitary 1949 Class 232U1

mention a mechanical stoker for the fireman's comfort. The SNCF, though, had long since standardised mechanical firing on its biggest types. To these the final addition, in 1947, was a standard 4-8-2, the 241P, a refined version of the pre-war PLM 4-8-2 class.

The Nord 4-6-4s, as well as the two semi-streamlined Krupps-built three-cylinder Class 10 express passenger Pacifics supplied in 1957 to West Germany's newly-formed Deutsche Bundesbahn, were born too late for the scope to flex their muscles fully. Broadly speaking, where any devastated or war-weary track had been thoroughly rehabilitated, it was to make paths straight for new diesels or for the electrifiers.

Germany

Europe was propelled into the First World War by its railways, both figuratively and literally. The plans which the Russians and Germans in particular had been drafting ever since the countries' knowledge of the ultimate certainty of impending war were fundamentally reliant on the deployment of their men and material by a gigantic, precisely time-tabled railway operation over a period of days. Thus the signal to set one juggernaut rolling immediately had to be countered by the launch of another. Both operations were so intensive that neither side could afford brinkmanship. For 16 days at the start of August 1914 the Hohenzollern Bridge over the Rhine at Köln, for example, carried a westward train on average every 10 minutes. The Germans' Schlieffen Plan, under which their northern armies were to head for the Belgian coast before veering southward to Paris, was to be mounted with an inaugural rail timetable covering 16 days.

Germany alone imposed total military control on its railways for the duration. The varying degrees of overall direction applied elsewhere were, however, effective enough to call into question the sense of reverting to the *status quo ante* of fragmented railway systems after the Armistice.

As for the defeated Powers, the terms of the 1919 Treaty of Versailles were draconian. The national Reichsbahn in which Germany's 1920 Weimar Constitution vested the country's railways was much less than the sum of the pre-war State systems. The 1,907km (1,224 miles) of railway in Alsace-Lorraine had to be returned to France, confronting the French with an operating problem, as they had been methodically reorganised and resignalled for German right-hand running; the French ultimately built some flying junctions as the least expensive way to pass trains unchecked to and from the adjoining areas where left-hand working was standard. Over 4,731km (2,940 miles) in the east had to be ceded to Poland; the Belgians took almost 161km (100 miles) in Eupen and Malmèdy, the Danes over 241km (150 miles) in Schleswig. Besides being obliged to surrender sufficient locomotives and rolling stock to operate these reclaimed railways, the Germans had to make good all the Allied equipment they had appropriated (and in most cases run into total disrepair) or destroyed. Claims under the latter totalled no fewer than 5,000 locomotives, 15,000 passenger coaches and 135,000 freight wagons. Every item the Germans surrendered in restitution had to be of the latest design, and in perfect order. Allied inspectors at the hand-over points made sure that the locomotives fulfilled the specification by putting them through trial runs. The bulk of these transactions were not completed until 1920 because a certain amount of the material offered was rejected. The final reshuffle was not approved until 1924.

Desperately short of equipment and of coal, and with a good deal of its fixed plant decrepit, the Reichsbahn started life with a rail system close to operational collapse in many areas. The recovery of German industry was a high priority, however, and restoration of railway efficiency was deemed to be its prerequisite; thus large-scale railway investment was quickly put in hand. At the same time rail freight rates and fares were pegged for industry's benefit, so that by 1923 the Reichsbahn was spending a phenomenal seven times as much as it was earning. Unification of the system and its urgent need for new traction

and rolling stock were a stimulus to make the most of such an opportunity by perfecting new technology.

The Reichsbahn was taken out of supreme German control and made a limited company, the Reichsbahn Gesellschaft, in 1923, under the authority of a supreme Reparations Commission. It was forced to make an annual contribution to German reparations payments and compelled to raise its charges substantially so that this obligation would be covered. The Reichsbahn was not returned to exclusively German management until 1930.

The standard German express passenger Pacific took shape after the 1920 amalgamation of the former railway systems into the unitary Reichsbahn. Pre-war Germany then had been generally content with Atlantics as its principal express passenger power, with mass production of a sturdy, uncomplicated mixed traffic 4-6-0 with just two simple-expansion cylinders, rather than an advance in sophisticated multi-cylinder compound design planned for specialised express duty. Between 1906 and 1921, the Prussians acquired an extraordinary 3,370 of this P8 class, one of Europe's classics that was also adopted by other

Class P8 No 038.382 at Horb in July 1972

Class P8 4-6-0

Country of origin: Germany
Railway: Royal Prussian Union Railway (KPEV)
Date: 1906
Length overall: 18.592m (61ft)
Total weight: 78,409kg (172,500lb)
Cylinders: two 575 × 630mm (22.6 × 24.8in)
Driving wheels: 1.75m (5ft 9in)
Axle load: 17,727kg (39,000lb)
Fuel: 5,000kg (11,000lb)
Grate area: 2.58m² (27.8sq ft)
Water: 21,338 litres (4,700 Imp gal/5,700 US gal)
Heating surface: 143.3m² (1,542sq ft)
Superheater: 58.9m² (634sq ft)
Steam pressure: 12kg/cm² (170.6psi)

railways and which was still widely active well into the second half of the century.

Such dedication to an all-purpose machine was largely attributable to the lack of sparkle in German train speed at the time. At the outbreak of the First World War the comparatively few trains timed at 81km/h (50mph) or even more between stops were largely accounted for by the two dozen which the Prussian State ran daily over the 162.5km (101 miles) between Berlin and Halle in 110 minutes at a mean speed of 89km/h (55mph). Elsewhere, pace was hobbled by the close spacing of significant towns that warranted frequent calls, and not least by the determination of many of them to preserve and exercise a right that they had insisted upon at the German railways' construction, to be served by every train on their main line.

Thus when the postwar Reichsbahn cast about for some existing types to extend as a stopgap replenishment of its locomotive fleet, desperately depleted by the war damage, post-war reparations and a backlog of repairs, the only inherited Pacific design that met a national, low axle-load express passenger specification was the former Bavarian State's own Maffei-built four-cylinder compound Class S3/6. This was a 186.7cm (6ft 1.5in) driving-wheel machine, though in 1912-13 the Bavarians had built 18 of a variant with 200.7cm (6ft 7in) wheels for its München to Würzburg line via Nurnberg.

That was the only route on which the Bavarian system countenanced a speed of even 113km/h (70mph), further evidence of the mostly pedestrian pace of German rail travel in the Edwardian years. The Reichsbahn certainly initially expected to find types suitable for national standardisation from amongst its heritage of 350 different classes, subject to some modification, particularly to maximise use of some standard components within the group. None thoroughly satisfied the operating specifications that had sought equal competence in the flat plains of North Germany and over the sharply graded and often tortuous routes in the south and west of the country, so limited further manufacture of certain reasonably acceptable State railway types had to be pursued as an interim measure. Meanwhile, a council of Reichsbahn and manufacturing industry engineers drafted a series of new designs.

Though the designs were in theory a committee exercise, they all had the authoritative stamp of the Reichsbahn's traction chief, R P Wagner, another of the giants of European steam's final half-century.

The first standard German Pacific of 1925 was produced in two-cylinder simple Class 01 and four-cylinder compound Class 02 options for practical comparison. The outcome confirmed majority opinion in Berlin that the advances in simple expansion had cancelled out any profit from the higher cost of compounding. The 02s were eventually rebuilt as simple expansion engines and the entire standard range was erected on the basic theme of high boiler pressure, simple expansion (mostly two, but in some cases three-cylinders),

No 01.169 moves off to run on shed at Lichtenfels in June 1968; 231 of the class 01 4-6-2s were built prior to the Second World War, and it was withdrawn from service in 1973

superheating, with long-travel valves and also high-mounted boilers and running plates to simplify maintenance access to moving parts. The Reichsbahn's standard designs made a profound impression on other European railway managements, several of which but above all those of Poland, Bulgaria, Yugoslavia and Turkey, had near-replicas of certain German types built in quantity for their own systems.

The Reichsbahn's civil engineers improved their track to such effect that Wagner's team could build their first Pacifics up to a 19.7 tonne (19.39 ton) axle-loading.

German high speed was not the sole preserve of diesel traction in the second half of the 1930s. In 1936 the streamlined Class 05 4-6-4s were allocated to new morning and evening five-car trains between Berlin and Hamburg with which they had to average 118.6km/h (73.7mph) eastbound, making 119.4km/h (74.2mph) westbound non-stop. The Berlin-Hamburg schedules set for the Reichsbahn's 05 4-6-4s excelled the best attained with British steam.

The most rigidly regulated industry was without question Germany's. Perfection of new eight and ten-coupled types under the Reichsbahn's standardisation programme of the 1930s had the Third Reich's war machine better supported with heavy freight power than that of any European combatant.

Nonetheless the Wehrmacht's deep thrusts both to the eastward and westward generated a massive demand for still more traction to serve the railways that had been overrun, and that in most cases had suffered depredations to their locomotive stock in the process. The outcome of this was the most profuse production run of a single locomotive type in world history. The Class 50 2-10-0 design of the Reichsbahn's standard range was revised as the Class 52, the 'Kriegslok', a simplified form that eschewed frills, using every conceivable method of man-hour economy in construction. With this was paired a variant with heavier axle-loading, the Class 42, and between 1942 and 1945 around 10,000 of the two types were put together in a score of works in occupied Czechoslovakia, Austria, Belgium and Poland as well as in Germany itself. In one month alone, September 1943, the output of Class 52 was 505. US production of spartan Class S160 2-8-0s and so called 'MacArthur' 2-8-2s, and the British manufacture for ship-

A 2-10-0 Class 44 at speed, with a consignment of iron ore

ment to war zone railways of Stanier's LMS 2-8-0 and later of Riddles' elemental 2-8-0 and 2-10-0 designs, were nowhere near as intensive.

After the War, every European mainland railway it had involved confronted awesome problems of reconstruction. For the Germans they were aggravated by the division of the Third Reich. This split a railway system developed on an east-west traffic axis into two independent networks, the newly formed Deutsche Bundesbahn (DB) in the west and the residual Deutsche Reichsbahn (DR) in the east, each of which had now to adapt to primarily north to south traffic flows. The great trunk routes of the Third Reich, such as Berlin-Hamburg, were severed by the new frontier between West and East Germany and denuded of most of their traffic. Conversely, north-south routes such as Köln-Mainz-Frankfurt and from Hamburg to München, via Hannover and Stuttgart all within West Germany, were to have thrust on them a weight of intercity passenger and freight business for which their infrastructure was clearly totally inadequate.

The first European impetus to the design of a purpose-built high-speed steam locomotive came from the trade association of German locomotive builders. On Christmas Eve 1931 this body advised the Reichsbahn that it was convinced that the need of such a machine would soon be inescapable, was independently embarking on preliminary studies, and also invited the Reichsbahn's traction and rolling stock bureau to collaborate. The Reichsbahn's initial reaction was lukewarm. It was alive to the need of more pace to combat the new threat from the air at the upper end of the passenger market, but felt it had that threat covered with the emerging plan for lightweight diesel streamliners. The railway therefore limited its interest to support for the design exercise with the construction of a single prototype as the ultimate but as yet undated end-product. Wagner, the Reichsbahn's motive power chief, was convinced from the start that the specification was best met by a 4-6-4 development, with bigger fireboxes and enlarged boiler heating surfaces of existing Class 01 and 03 Pacifics taking shape in the Reichsbahn's standard range. That was what eventually materialised, but not until folios of the competitive designs which Wagner's colleagues and superiors preferred to solicit from the six major German builders had been sifted and dismissed. They were an exotic collection, including a basically Stephensonian 4-6-4 with 250.2cm (8ft 2.5in) driving wheels, a steam turbine or two and numerous cab-in-front creations, since one school of thought was convinced that at the higher speeds in mind the engine crew must have a panoramic forward view.

So well over two years had elapsed before a Borsig proposal that closely reflected Wagner's original idea was committed to metal in 1934. By then so much had been spent in research and development that the Reichsbahn upped the building order to three locomotives, but it promptly nullified some of the economics of this by ordering the third as a cab-in-front type that was mechanically fired with pulverised coal to save the inverted layout's handicap of a lengthy feed from the tender to firebox at the front end. The aim was to determine whether the advantages of a front-end cab outweighed its accompanying complications. They did not: No 05.003 made no mark on history and was soon rebuilt.

Not so Nos 05.001 and 05.002. The second of these comprehensive three-cylinder 4-6-4s with streamlining, 229.9cm (7ft 6.5in)

driving wheels, a high 129kg (285lb) boiler pressure and very spacious firegrate was spurred up to a world steam speed record of 200.4km/h (124.5mph) on all but level track near Berlin in May 1936. That was a well-prepared and publicised demonstration with a four-coach load of Third Reich functionaries, staged to add a technological glitter to the show of physical strength put on by Hitler's re-occupation of the Rhineland the previous March.

The two made just as much impression on the new pair of morning and evening Berlin-Hamburg expresses to which they were assigned in October 1935. These five-car trains, put on to supplement the limited seating of the diesel streamliners, were at first timed over the whole 286.6km (178.1 miles) between the two cities at an average of 122.8km/h (76.3mph) when eastbound and 124.6km/h (77.4mph) westbound, but with a maximum speed limited to 145km/h (90mph) that was too demanding, and in 1936 the schedules were eased out to a still spectacular 118.6 and 119.4km/h (73.7 and 74.2mph).

By 1939 the Reichsbahn had lifted the steam speed up a notch to 150km/h (93mph) on several suitably signalled and

Class 01.[10] 4-6-2

Railway: German Federal Railway (DB)
Date:1939, rebuilt 1953
Length overall: 24.13m (79ft 2in)
Total weight: 110,800kg (244,000lb) excluding tender
Cylinders: three 500 × 600mm (19.7 × 23.5in)
Driving wheels: 2m (6ft 6.7in)
Axle load: 20,200kg (44,500lb)
Fuel: 10,000kg (22,000lb)
Grate area: 3.96m² (42.6sq ft)
Water: 38m³ (8,400 Imp gal/ 10,000 US gal)
Heating surface: 206.5m² (2,223sq ft)
Superheater: 96.2m² (1,035sq ft)
Steam pressure: 16kg/cm² (227.6psi)

DB built two three-cylinder Pacifics for express passenger services before reverting to the upgrading of much of its prewar steam power. The first engines to be altered were 55 Pacifics of the Class 01.[10]

upgraded trunk routes and had embarked on mass-production of streamlined Pacifics, 55 of Class 01.10 and 60 of Class 03.10 (two huge streamlined 4-8-4s, Class 06, were also produced). In the last pre-war summer, however, steam-hauled Reichsbahn trains were less dazzlingly timed than they had been in the middle of the decade. Even the Berlin-Hamburg flyers were marginally decelerated.

Great Britain

British express services were easily the fastest in the world during the 1880s. By the early years of the twentieth century, with the network virtually complete, the prospects for growth and prosperity beckoned. The number of passengers was steadily growing; St Pancras station, which handled Midland Railways' traffic, showed a rise from 650,000 annually at the turn of the century to 880,000 in 1913, an increase of 33%.

The railway companies now turned their attention to the operation of trains of increased comfort, and necessarily also, of increased weight.

The large-boilered 4-4-0 was firmly established as the type of express locomotive most likely to be built in large numbers in the immediate future, but the increases in traffic and train weights were already emphasising that something bigger would soon be needed. By the close of the nineteenth century, both the Great Northern Railway (GNR) and Lancashire and Yorkshire Railway (L&YR) had introduced 4-4-2 Atlantic locomotives, and the North Eastern Railway (NER) was

An Atlantic Class 4-4-2 of LNER

soon operating 4-6-0 passenger trains, which were to point the way for future development.

In 1903, J F McIntosh of the Caledonian Railway built two 4-6-0s which were claimed to be Britain's largest and most powerful express engines. They were intended for the heavy west coast expresses over the Carlisle to Glasgow route. He built a slightly larger version, the 903 or Cardean Class, in 1906. Number 903 *Cardean* was used almost every day on the 2pm express out of Glasgow on the first stage of the journey to

One of only ten true City Class 4-4-0 locomotives to be built

London's Euston, and back from Carlisle on the corresponding train down. In 1909, *Cardean* sustained a speed of 70.8km/h (44mph) up the 1.25% (1 in 125) gradient climb to the Shap Summit, hauling 396.28 tonnes (390 tons). This was a feat unmatched in 1909, but there was little further development of the 4-6-0 in England.

The Great Western Railway (GWR) had an agreement with the London and South Western, whereby the Plymouth-London ocean mail was carried by the former and passengers by the latter. Both companies were keenly aware of the prestige value of claiming the fastest

journey, which in 1903 was held by the Great Western with a time of 233.5 minutes for the 397km (246.54-mile) Plymouth to Paddington journey. Early in 1904 racing began in earnest, and on 9 May City Class 4-4-0 *City of Truro* passed 100mph (161km/h) with an ocean mail special.

These record runs were made with lighter weight special trains, but Great Western also claimed the fastest scheduled services in the world. In 1902, the daily service between London and Birmingham was run at 89.4km/h (55.5mph); in 1903, a service to Bristol was scheduled at 96.6km/h (60mph), and in 1904 the introduction of the *City of Truro* on the 'Cornish Riviera Express', at the time the longest non-stop run in the world, gave a mean 89.4km/h (55.5mph) for the 395.3km (245.5-mile) journey.

The growing weight of these services now called for more powerful locomotives and in this the Great Western followed the example of the Caledonian Railway. Its 4-6-0s, however, were to be designed by George Churchwood, conceivably the greatest railway engineer Britain produced in the twentieth century, who after studying contemporary practice on both European and north American

Saint class 4-6-0

Railway: Great Western Railway (GWR)
Date: 1902
Length overall: 19.209m (63ft 0.25in)
Total weight: 114,090kg (251,000lb)
Cylinders: two 470 × 762mm (18.5 × 30in)
Axle load: 18,863kg (41,500lb)
Fuel: 6,136kg (13,500lb)
Grate area: 2.52m² (27.1sq ft)
Water: 15,890 litres (3,500 Imp gal/4,200 US gal)
Heating surface: 171m² (1,841sq ft)
Superheater: 24.4m² (263sq ft)
Steam pressure: 15.8kg/cm² (225psi)
Adhesive weight: 56,818kg (125,000lb)
Tractive effort: 11,066kg 24,395lb)

*The first production batch of 19 were named after characters in Sir Walter Scott's Waverley novels and appeared in 1905, following three prototypes, including the original **William Dean**. In 1906, 10 were built which were all named after Ladies, and include the first British locomotive to incorporate a modern superheater, the **Lady Superior**. These were followed first by 20 Saints, in 1907*

railways produced his prototype, No 98, in 1903.

He introduced the continental Belpaire firebox, combined with a new type of tapered boiler, using the American style of outside cylinders and also the cylinders and valve gear that allowed the freest passage of steam. He also increased efficiency by using longer-stroke pistons. What evolved were the two-cylinder Saint and four-cylinder Star classes, both of which were outstanding engines and which were further developed into the famous Castle Class of 1921. The Churchwood 4-6-0s took over much of the heavier work on the west of England line.

The first of the Castles appeared in 1923. Named *Caerphilly Castle*, it was the first of a type that was to prove so successful that modified versions of it were still being built in 1950.

In service the Castles were able to achieve a record-breaker with the Cheltenham Flyer in June 1932, when the 124km (77 miles) between Swindon and Paddington were covered at an average speed of 132km/h (81.7mph).

During the First World War, the railways had been brought under Government control, and afterwards there were moves to nationalise them, but in the face of opposition from the

companies a policy of compulsory amalgamation was begun, and a wholesale reorganisation took place of the British railway companies.

A total of 120 companies was formed into just four main groups, of which the Great Western was the only one that retained its name. The other three groups were the London, Midland and Scottish (this now included the London and North Western, Midland and Caledonian as its major constituents); the London and North Eastern (including the North Eastern, Great Northern and Great Eastern); and the Southern (bringing together the London and South Western and the other companies serving the

Castle Class No 7018

Castle class 4-6-0

Railway: Great Western Railway (GWR)
Date: 1923
Length overall: 19.683m (65ft 2in)
Total weight: 128,863kg (283,500lb)
Cylinders: four 406 × 660mm (16 × 26in)
Driving wheels: 2.045m (6ft 8.5in)
Axle load: 20,227kg (44,500lb)
Fuel: 6,136kg (13,500lb)
Grate area: 2.81m² (30.3sq ft)
Water: 18,160 litres (4,000 Imp gal/4,800 US gal)
Heating surface: 190m[2] (2,049sq ft)

One of the 74 King Arthur Class 4-6-0 locomotives

King Arthur class 4-6-0

Railway: Southern Railway (SR)
Date: 1925
Length overall: 20.244m (66ft 5in)
Total weight: 141,136kg (310,500lb)
Cylinders: two 521 × 711m (20.5 × 28in)
Driving wheels: 2.007m (6ft 7in)
Axle load: 20,454kg (45,000lb)
Fuel: 5,000kg (11,000lb)
Grate area: 2.8m² (30sq ft)
Water: 22,700 litres (5,000 Imp gal/6,000 US gal)
Heating surface: 174.5m² (1,878sq ft)

south coast area).

Following this huge amalgamation, rationalisation of motive power must inevitably take place.

Churchwood's influence also began to make itself felt, even outside of the Great Western. On the Southern Railway, the ex-London and South Western King Arthur class 4-6-0s were incapable of meeting 88.6km/h (55mph) schedules with the increased loads of up to 500-tonne (492.1-ton) trains now necessary to meet the current traffic demands. The four-cylinder 4-6-0s of the Lord Nelson class resulted, following studies of the Castle class, and were employed to cope with the heaviest expresses.

William Stanier, who had been employed by the Great Western, was appointed chief mechanical engineer of the London, Midland and Scottish and was responsible for the amazingly capable Black Five 4-6-0, of which no fewer than 842 were built between 1934 and 1951.

Meanwhile, the trend in the biggest passenger engines had been towards the Pacific type, whose pair of rear carrying wheels allowed a bigger firebox to be used. The first British Pacific had been produced by Churchwood in 1908, but this example, the *Great Bear,*

Above: Lord Nelson Class, which had Walschaert's valve gear between the frames, together with the four cylinders

proved to be too heavy for most of the Great Western track. There was then a long gap before further examples of Pacific-type locomotives were built, and then this was possible only by taking advantage of a loophole in the 1921 Railways Act. The Act, which enforced the grouping, allowed the

Poster used by LNER to launch the 'Silver Jubilee' with the first of the A4s in 1935

companies a period of preliminary organisation. The North Eastern and the Great Northern both took full advantage of this to produce their own designs, the former by Sir Vincent Raven and the latter by Nigel Gresley. Gresley became the chief mechanical engineer of the new group, and while only five of the Raven Pacifics were built, his own prototypes formed the basis of an impressive series.

Once again the influence of the Castles was apparent in the new designs, and comparative trials between the two types in 1925 convinced Gresley that the higher boiler pressure that was employed in the Churchwood design was worthwhile in terms of economical working.

Production of A3 Pacifics was begun in 1928 and the new engines were spectacularly successful. In March 1935, on a special trial run between Kings Cross and Newcastle-upon-Tyne, the A3 *Papyrus* covered well over half of the 864.6km (537-mile) round trip at a good 128.8km/h (80mph), reaching a maximum speed of 173.9km/h (108mph) and recorded an average of 112.3km/h (69.8mph) for the return trip to Newcastle.

It was then decided to institute a four-hour schedule for the Newcastle service, and in order to ensure that this could be achieved in normal traffic, a new design of Pacific, the A4 was ordered. The first of the new engines, *Silver Link*, made its public *début* on a special trial in September 1935, when more records were broken, with a top speed of 181.1km/h (112.5mph) being recorded.

To go with the specially streamlined A4s, new trains of streamlined stock were produced for the four-hour Silver Jubilee service. By this stage the London and North Eastern and London, Midland and Scottish had become involved in a new version of the famous 1895 races to Scotland, when the agreement that ended those contests came to an end in 1932.

In 1933, the LMS introduced the new Princess class Pacifics for the Royal Scot service between London and Glasgow, and following the introduction of the streamlined Silver Jubilee train the company set about producing its own streamlined Pacifics. The first of the new engines were built for a new service inaugurated in 1937 and named the Coronation Scot,

Above: *LNER Class A3 Pacific*

Below: *without doubt, the Class A4 streamlined 4-6-2 is the most popular and probably the best steam locomotive ever built*

which was scheduled to cover the 645.6km (401 miles) between London and Glasgow in 6.5 hours.

By this time, the London and North Eastern had introduced a six-hour service run between London and Edinburgh, the Coronation, which involved speeds of 161km/h (100mph) on many occasions, and in 1938, under the pretext of carrying out braking trials, an all-out attempt was made at a new speed record.

The engine involved was the A4 Pacific *Mallard*, and on 3 July 1938 a speed of 202.9km/h (126mph) was reached with the Silver Jubilee train and a special dynamometer car to record the performance. The record was established, but only at the expense of severe overheating, and the following year the Second World War intervened to put a stop to any further attempt at increased speeds on the Scottish services.

The achievements of the streamlined Pacifics could not fail to impress and influence other designers. One who was particularly open to such influence was Oliver Bulleid, who, as Gresley's assistant, had been closely involved in the evolution of the A4's stream-lined form. He came up with a new 4-6-2 design in which he had combined a boiler of high steam-raising capacity with three cylinders and a chain-driven valve gear running in a closed oil bath. Bulleid did not streamline the engines but he did employ air-smoothing, whereby the whole engine was enclosed in metal sheeting. His first mixed-traffic locomotive appeared in 1941 and, proving capable of the highest speeds required, was produced in two classes; the Merchant Navy class with the larger engine, and the Battle of Britain and West Country classes which had a smaller engine.

Two days before the outbreak of the Second World War on 3 September 1939, the Government took control of the four main-line railways, the London Passenger Transport Board and five smaller railways.

In the first four days of the War, the new Railway Executive Committee was able to arrange the evacuation from London of over 600,000 civilians, most of them children, on 1,577 special trains; plus more than 700,000 others, from 17 other major cities in England and Scotland, on a further 2,246 trains. This must be one of the most remarkable feats in any railway's history.

Yet another of the railway's wartime successes was in the

No 35011 General Steam Navigation, *an unrebuilt Merchant Navy Class*

evacuation of Dunkirk, when between 27 May and 4 June nearly 300,000 British soldiers rescued from the beaches of Dunkirk were transported in 565 special trains from the ports to London. The railways had been told to expect 30,000 men and it is a credit to the entire staff that an extraordinary feat of improvisation enabled them to carry it all through successfully.

Another incredible fact is that during wartime the freight tonnage had increased dramatically; in 1943 it had risen 43%

over the peacetime volume, despite the shortage of staff and movement having to be confined primarily to night-time, with little or no light. The task for the rail network was prodigious; no less than 460 trains were needed to take the men to the new airfields in East Anglia. Each 1000-bomber raid required 28 fuel trains and 8 bomb-carrying trains, and from 26 March 1944 until the start of D-Day on 6 June the railways had to run 24,459 special trains, of which 3,636 were scheduled in the week before D-Day. The weeks after D-Day were yet more frantic, with 18,000 special trains scheduled in the first four weeks.

The state of the railways at the end of the war in 1945 can hardly be imagined; not only was their stock and track barely usable, but they were poorly compensated for their efforts by the Government.

The Labour government soon nationalised the railways in 1948 and new groupings came into effect. The Western Region took over the old GWR, and the Southern Region suffered little change. The LMS lost territory in the north to become the London Midland Region, and the LNER also lost its northern section, which together with that from LMS formed the new Scottish Region. In the south, the LNER was split into the Eastern and the North Eastern Regions which were later re-united to become the Eastern Region, in 1967.

Responsibility for the track, rolling stock and motive power was vested in the Railway Executive Board. This decided to develop a new range of stan-

dard and mainly mixed-traffic steam locomotives, over seven power ranges up to express passenger Pacific status. These Class 9 2-10-0s proved very successful, and the last in the class, *Evening Star*, was the last steam locomotive built for British Railways (BR).

However, it was not until 1955 that the railways finally got the go-ahead for the much-needed modernisation plan, heralding the end for the steam locomotive, and inevitably its replacement by either diesel or electric locomotives.

In 1958, BR had had 16,108 steam locomotives; five years later, the number had shrunk to 7,050. On 11 November 1965, the last regular steam-hauled passenger train left Paddington, and three years later the last regular goods service to be operated by steam also came to an end.

Britain's farewell to steam took the shape of the Class 9 2-10-0s

Italy

Italy is yet another European country where the original railways were built by individual states, and electrification had been begun at an early stage. It was only in 1870 that the unification of Italy was achieved, and the old state systems continued to operate until after the First World War.

Perhaps the best-known fact about Italian railways is that Mussolini made the trains run on time, though this is actually as much a myth as might be expected. The credit actually belongs to Carlo Crova, who in the 1920s˙ was responsible, as general manager of the new State system, for the old Adriatic, Mediterranean and Sicilian systems, and who succeeded in imposing order and punctuality on them: the *fascisti* just happened to be handily placed at the time to take credit.

Among the locomotives that have operated on Italian railways are some unusual designs. In 1900 the Plancher type with the cab in front of the boiler was

The Class 640 2-6-0 dates from 1907, just after the formation of the Italian State Railways (FS). A total of 188 of the class were built; No 640.071 is seen here at Bard Fort in June 1971

built to make life easier for the crew in the narrow tunnels of the Adriatic main line, and in 1937 also, another cab-in-front design was produced by Attilio Franco, whose concern was with improving boiler efficiency. Franco's ideas were developed by Piero Crosti into a distinctive type of boiler which carried feedwater tanks alongside the main boiler, and led the exhaust gases through these to the chimneys at the sides of the boiler.

This boiler was used on a series of 83 modified locomotives and the 743 class, among other Italian types, and was used on ten of the British BR9 standard type 2-10-0s. As with other innovations of this period, however, it appeared too late for a full evaluation of its worth, though the extra complication of construction and maintenance would probably outweigh the savings of 10% in fuel, except where coal was in short supply.

The last pre-war word on rail passenger speed issued from Italy. Before the First World War, travel on Italian trunk routes had been purgatorially slow. From Naples to Milan, for instance, took at best 17 hours and that only if the train ran on time: but punctuality was more observed in planning than in

No 685.196 at Venezia Mestre in September 1981

actual performance. Between the wars, however, the Fascist *régime* had revolutionised the trunk routes, so much so that by the 1939 summer the same journey of 842km (523 miles) could be achieved in eight hours.

Under Mussolini, all of the country's intercity passenger services were transformed not only by acceleration, which generally halved the end-to-times of the best trains, but by massive expansion of train frequencies, up to as much as 114% between Rome and Naples, although this was accomplished largely by widespread electrification.

Class 685 2-6-2

Railway: State Railways (FS)
Date: 1912
Length overall: 20.57m (67ft 6in)
Total weight: 120,400kg (265,362lb)
Cylinders: four 420 × 650mm (16.5 × 25.5in)
Driving wheels: 1.85m (6ft 0.75in)
Axle load: 16,000kg (35,500lb)
Fuel: 6,000kg (13,500lb)
Grate area: 3.5m² (38sq ft)
Water: 22m³ (4,040 Imp gal/4,842 US gal)
Heating surface: 178.6m² (1,922sq ft)
Superheater: 48.5m² (516sq ft)
Steam pressure: 12kg/cm² (171psi)
Adhesive weight: 47,000kg (103,500lb)

Spain

Both Spanish and Portuguese railways use a gauge of 167.6cm (5ft 6in). Spanish railways were initially built by both the various states and by private concerns, but all using imported locomotives.

As soon as Europe was used to the bulk of a Pacific at the front end of an express train than one or two railways moved up a locomotive size. The 1925 choice of Spain's Norte Railway for a relatively quite small-wheeled 4-8-2, forerunner of what became typically Spanish express passenger power for steam's remaining decades, was quite under-

A 242 Class 4-8-4 of RENFE, one of ten locomotives built in Barcelona; they were the last European express steam locomotives built to run on electrified main line

standable, for Spanish main lines were frequently fierce switchbacks where extra adhesion of a fourth coupled axle would be an asset.

Spanish railway operation was dominated by just four companies, which survived considerable financial strains till the depredations of the Spanish Civil War had made a State takeover inevitable in 1943, when the national system, RENFE, was created.

Conditions on Spanish railways are often similar to those in Austria, with long-distance routes and many mountain sections, and the 4-8-0 was adopted at an early stage. Subsequent designs have typically had eight-coupled driving wheels, with two of four leading and trailing wheels. A distinctive example is the F2001 class 4-8-4, a big and powerful type first built in 1955 and used to operate heavy passenger services.

Switzerland

Sharing frontiers with both France and Germany, the Alpine republic of Switzerland has developed one of the most varied railway systems in the world. Although Switzerland would not appear to be the most likely candidate for an extensive railway network, one of the first acts of the new government formed by the country's federation in 1848 was to ask Robert Stephenson to advise on the creation of a national railway system, and the resulting Swiss system today is easily the busiest in Europe.

As far as power is concerned, electrification began early in the twentieth century, and was completed on the state system in 1960, but in the meantime some interesting steam operations were mounted. On the main lines there were high-speed services on the valley routes, while before being electrified in 1922 the line through the St Gotthard Tunnel, the independent Jura-Simplon line originally, demanded extremely powerful engines.

Perhaps most fascinating, however, are the narrow-gauge and rack systems used to reach the less accessible points on the railway map. In 1858, for the opening of the Hauenstein line,

which climbs 182.9m (600ft) in 10.1km (6.25 miles) between Sissach and Laufelfingen, the locomotive *Genf* was employed to haul the official train. The unusual system used to give much increased adhesion was developed by the Austrian engineer Engerth for use on the Semmering Pass, and involved carrying the frames of the tender ahead of the locomotive firebox, and using gears to drive the front pair of coupled tender wheels. The Swiss central railway used as many as 60 very similar locomotives during the later years of the nineteenth century.

The Swiss railway system must inevitably involve many impressive tunnels and bridges, while the narrow-gauge lines were common and rack railways came into their own. One railway which combined all four was the metre-gauge Furka-Oberalp, with a rack system over the steepest sections and an impressive viaduct leading to the Gringiols spiral tunnel. This line, too, has been electrified.

The last rack railway to be operated by steam was the Brienz to Rothorn line, which climbs over 1,676.4m (5,500ft) from the shores of Lake Brienz to the summit of the Rothorn. A striking feature of the rack

Class A3/5 4-6-0

Country of origin: Switzerland
Railway: Swiss Federal
Railways (SBB)
Date: 1913
Length overall: 18.64m (61ft 2in)
Total weight: 110,000kg
(243,000lb)
Cylinders: high-pressure, two
360 × 660mm (14.25 × 26in);
low-pressure, two 570 × 660mm
(22.5 × 26in)
Driving wheels: 1.78m (5ft 10in)
Axle load: 16,000kg (35,550lb)
Fuel: 7,000kg (15,500lb)
Grate area: 2.6m² (28sq ft)
Water: 17.8m³ (3,900 Imp gal/
4,700 US gal)
Heating surface: 129m² (1,389sq
ft)

*The most common 4-6-0 of the
Swiss Federal Railway was the
Class A3/5, of which 109
locomotives were built between
1902 and 1909, originally
without superheaters*

locomotives, which engage a
rack slid between the running
rails with a cog-wheel to obtain
traction, and which always
operate downhill on the cars, is
their canted bodies. These
enable them to remain roughly
horizontal on the steepest sections and prevent the forward
part of the firetubes from being
exposed by water running to
the back of the boiler. Early
rack locomotives often had vertical boilers for the same
reason.

Wagon-lits and Luxury Travel

In France, where the Wagon-Lits company had the exclusive dining-car concession, a level of cuisine was fashioned mostly for the upper end of the travel market and priced accordingly; as a result, restaurant cars were listed for only 158 daily trains.

The success of the Wagon-Lits company and the stimulus to expand its operation was patent, however, in the breadth of its sleeping-car operation in France. None of the British companies running overnight from London to the North offered a service to compare with that of the PLM. Every night the PLM was despatching 14 sleeping-car trains from Paris Gare de Lyons to the Riviera, the Alps and Italy.

From December 1922, those Gare de Lyons departures included a train that heralded the new, inter-war style of the European *train de luxe*, the 'Paris-Mediterranean'.

This and its companion, the new 'Calais-Mediterranean', were simultaneously inaugurated for the prodigious new market for premium-fare travel from Britain to the mainland, and the *débutants* of the Wagon-Lits company's first all-steel sleeping cars, liveried in gold-lined dark blue instead of the previous wooden-bodied cars' teak.

Each car embodied single and two-berth compartments – both exclusively first-class on this prestigious service – which were exquisitely finished internally with real mahogany panelling that extended to the lavatories; in some of those built, adjoining pairs of rooms shared an intervening dressing-room with wash-basin, which left room in each compartment for a comfortable armchair facing the berths. The status of travel by Wagon-Lits *train de luxe* in the 1920s was the natural medium for European diplomats to go about their business and for the nobility and *nouveaux-riches* to take their vacationing pleasure. This was obvious from the glittering company which assembled on Nice station to greet the first arrivals of the new trains. Everyone who counted in the Côte d'Azur's administration was mobilised as a matter of course, but the Crown Prince of Sweden and the Duke of Connaught, wintering on the coast at the time, joined many of the Riviera society's *élite* who felt it incumbent on them to repair to the station of their own accord to salute the incoming trains. The external colour of the new cars quickly earned these new trains the tag by which they are far better known, *train bleu*, though the title was not given the official stamp until 1949.

In the Depression years, the Calais train contracted to just two sleepers, run to Paris in the *Flèche d'Or* and worked from the Gare du Nord via the capital's Ceinture line for attachment to the *train bleu* at Gare de Lyons. Though its British trade declined, that same *train bleu* remained the acme of French travelling fashion

Dining car of a train de luxe *in 1912, the heyday of the luxury train*

throughout the inter-war years. In the height of the season it was an odds-on bet that at least some of the 'beautiful people' draped around the French capital's Ritz bar one night would the next be congregated in the chic Pullman-style lounge bar which the *train bleu* acquired after a few years in service. There cocktails and gossip ritually flowed for the first hour after the train's departure from Paris before the maître d'hôtel deferentially beckoned guests to a six-course *tour de force* in the adjoining diner.

Pullman and Wagon-Lits were now intimately associated in Europe under Lord

Davidson Dalziel. The 1920s were marked by his energetic expansion of Pullman services, many of them as exclusively Pullman trains, on both sides of the Channel. At the same time the Wagon-Lits business was developed both territorially and quantitatively, in the latter case to a significant degree by the construction from 1924 of sleeping cars specifically for the second-class passengers who had been admitted to the double-berth compartments of certain services since 1919. All this had swollen Dalziel's rolling stock resources by 1925 (Britain excluded) to a total of 1,739 cars of all kinds in commission, plus a total of 179 more sleepers, 85 diners and 96 Pullmans under construction. His companies' rail activity covered not only the greater part of Europe, but also the Middle East, North Africa and even the Far East, where the 'Trans-Siberian Express' had begun making a regular nine-day journey from Moscow to Kharbin and thence into China in 1903. The Russian Revolution of 1917 cut short that exercise at once, with the Wagons-Lits company stripped of all its rolling stock and other assets in Russia and totally uncompensated. From 1919, however, it operated the new

Below: *an advertisement for Wagon-Lits trains, which in the*

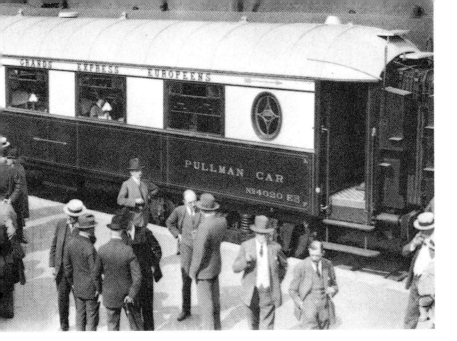

1920s opened services beyond western Europe

Above: *the inauguration of the* Flèche d'or *in 1926*

'Trans-Manchurian Express' from Tchita to Vladivostock, complementing this later with services from Harbin as far as Changchun and from Nanking to Peking, where it had its own hotel. At the end of the 1930s the company was still running 20 cars in the Far East.

By the mid-1930s, the railways in France were making shattering losses, increased by a further 15% loss in the first half of 1936. That summer the Popular Front Government of the Left swept to power. As already recorded, its natural response was nationalisation. Once that had been effected, the Popular Front *régime* mounted

a fresh co-ordination drive which resumed the transfer of break-of-gauge, where passengers changed to a broad-gauge sleeping and restaurant car 'Sud Express' for the remainder of their journeys to Madrid or Lisboa. The next step was to link the budding continental Pullman network with its British counterpart. That was also achieved in 1926 with the inauguration of the all-Pullman *Flèche d'Or* between Calais and Paris, and a complementary all-Pullman train run between London Victoria and Dover. The latter, inscrutably, was not named 'Golden Arrow' until 1929; some say the Southern's refusal to match the French train's name immediately was pure chauvinistic antipathy to honouring a foreign enterprise, since the 'golden' epithet was a tribute to the Wagon-Lits company in its jubilee year. The European schedules were dotted annually with a number of new Pullman trains in the remaining 1920s, though a few were commercial fiascos.

Pullman train working even extended to Egypt, where the Wagon-Lits company had had a foothold since the late nineteenth century. The successful operation of single cars during the earlier 1920s prompted the November 1929 creation of a thrice-weekly all-Pullman service, the 'Sunshine Express', between Cairo and Luxor. This built up a handsome Anglo-American tourist trade in the 1930s: the done thing was to make a round trip between the two cities by the Nile steamer one way and the Pullman the other. The 'Sunshine Express' died with the Second World War, but Wagon-Lits still ran sleeping-cars in Egypt until the early 1960s.

The Wagon-Lits company was debarred from operating any internal German services. Foiled in its post-war intrigues to destroy Mitropa, the similar company in which the Kaiser's Government vested Wagon-Lits' German-based assets in 1915, it had to be content with a spheres-of-influence pact with its rival. This allowed Wagon-Lits cars on international itineraries to transit the Reichsbahn, and Mitropa to run through to Dutch, Austrian, Swiss and Scandinavian destinations.

The most spectacular result was Mitropa's 1928 opening up of an alternative luxury route from England to one of Britain's most cherished havens, Switzerland, via the Hook of Holland, Köln and the Rhine Valley to Basle. Pullman-like in its concept and furnishing, the 'Rheingold' stung Wagon-Lits into a counter-attack within four weeks.

The riposte was a new train, also drawing its British clientèle from London and Harwich, then a night boat across the North Sea: the 'Edelweiss Pullman' from Antwerp, which gained Basle via Luxembourg and Strasbourg. The Swiss Federal gave the rivals strictly impartial treatment. At Basle it combined their respective Zurich and Lucerne portions into a pair of trains, eye-catching in their juxtaposition of the blue-and-cream mainland Pullman and purple-and-white 'Rheingold' liveries.

UNITED STATES OF AMERICA

By 1900, passenger trains on the US railway network were notable more for the distance they covered than for their speed. Well over 241,500km (150,000 miles) had been added to the 48,300km (30,000 miles) of route of 50 years earlier.

Traffic, revenue and earnings were all more than doubled between 1900 and 1913, but the Depression in 1913-1914 caused a small drop in traffic and a larger drop in income: there was far too much spare capacity, and in the two years to 1915 some 6% 24,135km (15,000 miles) of track were in receivership.

When the federal government assumed control in 1917, the men who had dominated the railroads during the years of expansion had gone. Gould, Vanderbilt, Morgan, Jim Hill and Ed Harriman had followed their visions, looting, building empires or rationalising, leaving as their legacies systems they created or destroyed.

Government control was extended, yet initially the railroads, while welcoming the standardisation of rates, had otherwise continued more or less as they pleased.

The government's conduct of the railroads was subsequently the subject of much controversy. Industry propaganda claimed that efficiency had deteriorated, that the policy of rerouting traffic from the Pennsylvania and the Baltimore and Ohio (B & O) onto the New York State trunk routes was misguided, and that the railroad's property was neglected. The Director-General of Railroads contended that efficiency was improved by standardisation of operation, and that the new equipment purchased and compensation paid amounted to a large government subsidy.

Whatever the truth of these conflicting claims, price and wage inflation had taken their toll. A doubling of operating revenue to $6 billion between 1914 and 1920 was accompanied by a four-fifths fall in net income to $100,000,000. The result was the Transportation Act of 1920, by which the railroads were returned to their prewar ownership, and included provision for low-interest federal loans and grants to be made available.

The Interstate Commerce Commission (ICC) produced a plan to consolidate the railroad network along the lines laid down by Congress. This was successfully opposed by the railroads, which then promptly embarked on consolidation, often by financial arrangements that avoided outright mergers, which the commission could block.

Following the government's assumption of control in the First World War, the US Railroad Administration began to rationalise the railroad supply industry with standard rolling stock designs, including 12 locomotive types.

One of these was a 2-8-8-2 Mallet based very closely on a Norfolk & Western (N & W) design, representative of the final phase of Mallet compound development in the USA. Total engine wheelbase was now stretched to 17.7m (58ft) to accommodate the two sets of 144.8cm (4ft 9in) driving wheels, and engine weight alone had climbed to 241 tonnes (237 tons). A boiler of 259.1cm (8ft 6in) diameter, squeezed chimney and domes to pimple height, and a mechanical stoker had the stamina to meet the demands of the 63.5cm (25in) low-pressure and 99.1cm (39in) high-pressure cylinders under the most relentless driving hand. The long, severe gradients and enormous trainloads of coal-hauling US railroads like the N & W subjected US locomotives to a sustained pounding rarely experienced in Europe. From the late 1920s onwards, most railroads were rejecting the Mallet for simple-expansion articulateds.

The Van Swerigen brothers of Cleveland acquired a series of railroads, including the Nickel Plate in 1916 and the Erie in 1923, while in 1924 the Pennsylvania bought a controlling interest in the N & W, a big coal carrier based in Roanoke, Virginia. The Pennsylvania went on to gain majorities in the stock of the Lehigh Valley, the Wabash and the Boston and Maine. This use of holding companies to circumvent the ICC rules was imitated by the Van Swerigens, who used their Allegheny Corporation to build up a 48,270km (30,000-mile) system, and it became so popular that companies organised by the eastern trunk lines spent over $300,000,000 on such activities in only 18 months during 1928-1929.

By now it was obvious, as even the president of the B & O admitted to a commission member, that the situation was beyond the ICC's control. The railroads had benefited to such an extent from the economic boom of the 1920s that the difficulties that had seemed so alarming in 1920 were forgotten, masked by the general growth of the traffic. Although route mileage declined slightly

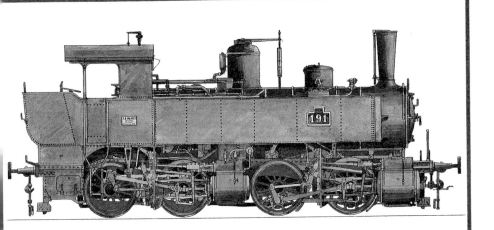

Above: *the Mallet compound used different cylinder sizes to drive two separate sets of driving wheels*

Below: *the Baltimore and Ohio Mallet, first of a range of giant Mallet engines to be built in the USA from 1904*

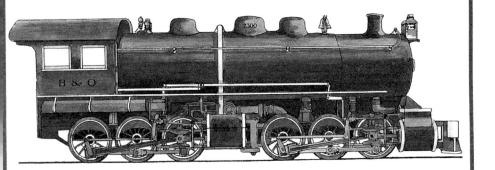

from its 1916 peak, track mileage had increased by some 160,000km (100,000 miles) to reach 579,240km (360,000 miles) in 1928. The railroads, though now acting corporately (except the Van Swerigen operation) rather than under the control of a few powerful individuals, appeared to return to the kind of anarchic power struggles that had caused such fatal weakness in the past.

A 'final' plan for the region, produced in 1929, was made redundant by the following year when revenues were down 15% on 1929. By 1932 revenues were down to half of their 1929 level. The number of passenger km/miles had already dropped by a third from their 1920 level of 72.4 billion km (45 billion miles) by 1928, largely as a consequence of the 15 million Model Ts that Ford had produced by then, and there were further large falls to come.

The railroads reacted with reductions in wages, dividends and numbers of employees; the government reacted with the National Transportation Committee (NTC), formed in 1932. This advised co-operation in order to eliminate wasteful competition. In 1933, the new Roosevelt administration produced the liberal Emergency Transportation Act, which endorsed the NTC's recommendations and called for a Federal Transport Commissioner and eastern, western and southern co-ordinating committees to carry them out, though at the same time limiting workforce reductions. In 1934 the Association of American Railroads (AAR) was formed to act as a national policy-making body.

The AAR and the ICC had soon reached agreement on a number of measures in what had become, for many railroads, a vital struggle to exist: however, traffic continued to decline, and by July 1938 no less than 39 major roads, representing over 25% of the total mileage, were in receivership, the Van Swerigen empire having been among the first casualties.

Reeling out of the 1930s, the railroads were greeted with a new Transportation Act in 1940, and this went even further toward meeting their demands. The land-grant railroads' longstanding obligation to carry government traffic at reduced rates was abolished; transport by water was added to the ICC's responsibilities; and a commitment was made to a national non-competitive policy for transport, though the new Act also called for preservation of the inherent advantages in the various modes of transport. The Act also established some new criteria for ICC approval of mergers, essentially based on consideration both of the public interest and an improved position for the railroads involved.

By the end of 1941 the railroads were once again a vital part of a war effort. This time, apart from a token three-week nationalisation at the end of 1944 to head off labour trouble, the railroads responded with a highly creditable display of cooperation with the Office of Defence Transportation, which made the drastic action of 1917 unnecessary; and also the two-way movement of war material and personnel helped avoid the crippling congestion at the ports that had been the trouble before.

Moreover, the railroads now showed financial judgment by applying the increased profits generated by the war traffic boom to reducing the fixed charges for interest on debts rather than squandering them on bumper dividends. The burden of debt had been a fetter on the railroads' fiscal freedom almost since their inception, and whereas formerly these debts had been regarded as permanent fixtures, a concerted drive towards repayment saw annual fixed charges reduced by $80,000,000 between 1940 and 1945. This was to stand them in good stead in the postwar years, when the improved credit enabled them to raise, without too much trouble, the $2 billion that would be needed to finance the death of the steam locomotive with wholesale dieselisation.

In 1896 John Wootten, general manager of the Philadelphia and Reading Railroad, had now developed that company's rather unstable 2-4-2 fast passenger engines into a new 4-4-2 wheel arrangement for its Atlantic City route, giving its name to this Atlantic type. The new engines proved capable of covering the 89.3km (55½ miles) from Camden to Atlantic City in just 60 minutes, and in special circumstances of an overall speed of 115 km/h (71.6mph).

The Pennsylvania RR also adopted the same type for its competing services. Pennsylvania Atlantics reached their highest development in the guise of the E6 class, first built in 1910, which included superheating. The invention of a German engineer, Wilhelm Schmidt, this involved collecting the steam in the normal way, then leading it through elements inside the firetubes so

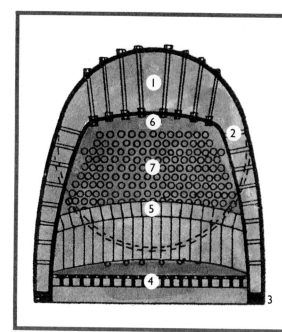

The Wootten firebox

Key

1 Stays
2 Screw stays
3 Foundation ring
4 Grate bars
5 Brick arch
6 Crown sheet
7 Tubes

that it was superheated to much greater temperatures and pressures before being admitted to the cylinders. With the addition of superheating in 1910, the E6 Atlantics developed 3,216kN (2,400hp), which for their weight of 111.77 tonnes (110 tons) made them among the most powerful locomotives ever built. They remained in use until after the Second World War.

The Pennsylvania Atlantics did not use Wootten fireboxes, having adopted the square-topped Belpaire type for its bituminous coal. The Reading

persevered with the Wootten, however, and in 1915 added a four-wheel trailing truck to produce a 4-4-4 type. Apart from the few high-speed machines built for special services with lightweight trains during the 1930s, this was the last flourish of the four-coupled passenger engine, the four-wheel trailing truck having yet to reach its true potential in other applications. For mainline passenger service the next type of major importance was the 4-6-2 Pacific.

A slightly earlier type, the 2-6-2 Prairie, had, like the 2-4-2 that preceded the Atlantic, proved unstable at high speeds, though the examples built during the 1900s were among the biggest passenger engines in the world at the time. The first Pacifics were built for the Missouri Pacific Railroad in 1902, thus providing their generic name. Again, it was the Pennsylvania which produced the most impressive examples of this engine type, and again the new wheel configuration was combined with other innovations to reach its highest peak of development.

The Pennsylvania's first Pacifics were the K2 class of 1907, which used the conventional arrangement of the cylinders sited outside the wheels of the leading truck, controlled by a Stephenson-type link motion carried between the wheels. These were replaced by another type of link motion, named after its Belgian inventor, Egide Walschaert, operating outside the wheels and which used more rugged piston valves. By 1914 the original K2 had been developed into the K4 with the addition of the Walschaert's gear. Although only 15% heavier than their predecessors, the K4s developed 33% more tractive effort, and were par-

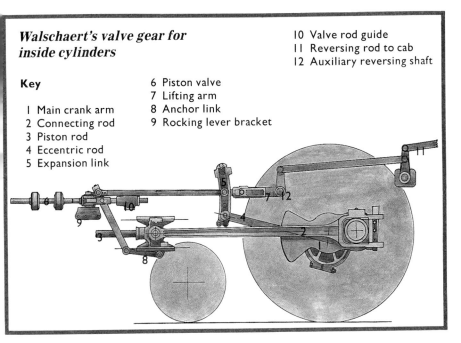

Walschaert's valve gear for inside cylinders

Key

1 Main crank arm
2 Connecting rod
3 Piston rod
4 Eccentric rod
5 Expansion link
6 Piston valve
7 Lifting arm
8 Anchor link
9 Rocking lever bracket
10 Valve rod guide
11 Reversing rod to cab
12 Auxiliary reversing shaft

ticularly useful on the Pennsylvania's heavily graded line from New York-Chicago. The addition of mechanical stokers in the 1920s allowed them to indulge to the full their appetite for fuel, which the stokers had to labour hard to satisfy, and as the weight of the trains increased they were provided with tenders carrying 90,847 litres (19,985 Imp/24,400 US gal) of water and 25.4 tonnes (25 tons) of fuel.

On the New York-Chicago run the Pennsylvania's great rival, the New York Central (NYC), had a longer but easier route alongside the Hudson river and Erie canal to the Great Lakes, rather than following the Pennsylvania on the direct route across the mountains. The NYC had also developed a series of Pacifics, starting in 1905, to take advantage of the easier route by running heavier trains. A series of NYC Pacifics culminated in the K5 class of 1925.

However, the K5s were fast approaching the very limits of the Pacific's capacity, and the demand for yet heavier locomotives was met in 1927 with the introduction of the first 4-6-4, known as the Hudson, from the location of the Central's main line out of New York. The four-wheel trailing truck was thus

adopted to allow a bigger grate to be used, and a development of Walschaert's valve gear, the Baker, was used on later models. Another feature of the Hudsons, which had earlier been fitted to the NYC Pacifics, was the inclusion of a small booster engine on the trailing truck to give extra power when starting.

The original J1 class Hudsons were developed over the years, and their ultimate form was reached in the streamlined J3s which achieved fame by hauling the prestige 'Twentieth Century Limited' between New York and Chicago in the late 1930s. The NYC, however, had a requirement for still greater power, and this was supplied in the form of the 4-8-4 Niagara type, developed from the series of 4-8-2 freight engines, the Mohawks, by the way of the L3 class 4-8-2s which had proved capable of speeds in excess of 129 km/h (80mph) even with the relatively small wheels

Above: *Class J1 4-6-4 No 5280 hauling the Empire State Express*

Below: *NYC's Niagara Class 4-8-4, also Alco-built, and employed on the New York-Chicago Twentieth Century Limited service*

commonly used for freight machines.

Meanwhile other railroads were developing other types of passenger engines; the Milwaukee had followed a similar progression from a series of 4-6-0 types in the 1890s. Both these and the succeeding Atlantic designs employed the Vauclain compound system, and in 1907 another Atlantic was produced with a balanced compounding system. This also used two high-pressure cylinders, but instead of having them in pairs, one above the other outside the leading truck wheels, the balanced system mounted the low-pressure pair inside the frames. From this position they drove the axle of the leading pair of driving wheels, which was cranked for the purpose, while the high-pressure cylinders drove the leading coupled wheels in the normal way.

Because of the additional complication, this system was never very popular on American railroads, and the more common Vauclain type was used again on the Milwaukee's last Atlantics in 1908. In 1910 the first class of Pacifics, the F3s, were introduced, to be followed by the F4 class in the next two years, and then the superheated F5 class: ultimately all

160 engines of the three classes were fitted with superheaters.

In 1929 a new class of locomotive was introduced, in the form of the 4-6-4. The new engines proved exceptionally fast, and on the 138km (86-mile) Chicago-Milwaukee route in July 1934 a special run produced the most remarkable speeds of 148.5km/h (92.3mph) averaged over a 105.5km (65.6 mile) section, with a maximum of 166.5km/h (103.5mph).

For the long hauls on the Pacific route, a more powerful type, the S1 4-8-4, was introduced, the first of which was produced by Baldwin in 1930. With a tractive force of over 28,123kg (62,000lb), compared with the 20,784kg (45,820lb) of the F6 class 4-6-4s, the S1s could haul the heaviest passenger trains.

During the 1930s the Milwaukee was to introduce its famous streamlined Hiawatha services, and for the Chicago-Minneapolis run, with a train of six cars, the American Locomotive Company (Alco) produced the A class 4-4-2 design in 1935. These proved capable of sustaining speeds of well over 161km/h (100mph), but as the popularity of the trains caused their size to be increased, first to nine and then to twelve cars, the F7 4-6-4s, first built in 1938, replaced them. These newer

No 4455, a Class GS-4 of 1941

Class GS-2 4-8-4

Railway: Southern Pacific
Railroad (SP)
Date: 1937
Length overall: 30.91m (101ft
5in)
Total weight: 401,364kg
(883,000lb)
Cylinders: two 648 × 813mm
(25.5 × 32in)
Driving wheels: 1.87m (6ft 1.5in)
Axle load: 31,330kg (68,925lb)
Fuel: 22,263 litres (4,900 Imp
gal/4,900 US gal) oil
Grate area: 8.4m² (90.4sq ft)
Water: 88,984 litres (19,600 Imp
gal/23,500 US gal)
Heating surface: 454m² (4,887sq
ft)
Superheater: 194m² (2,086sq ft)

engines could take the heavier
trains at maximum speeds of
over 193km/h (120mph), and
worked one of the fastest-ever
steam-hauled scheduled runs in
the world, the 130km/h (81mph)
Sparta to Portage section of
the Minneapolis to Milwaukee
route.

The need for both minimum
servicing and maintenance
became paramount as the locomotives had been developed to
such a peak of speed and power
that track and other limita-
tions, rather than locomotive
ability, had become the govern-
ing factor in the schedules. It
was against a background of
increasing competition from
diesel locomotives, one of the
attractions of which was their
greater availability, that the

New York Central produced its ultimate development of the Niagara type.

The designing brief was a 8,040kN (6,000hp) engine with a weight to horsepower ratio no higher than that of the 4-6-4s. In pursuit of this, a new design of boiler was adopted which omitted the steam dome to allow increased diameter; at the same time the firebox, steam passages and super-heater elements were made bigger, carbon steel was employed where appropriate, and roller bearings were adopted. Furthermore, to permit a full evaluation of the design, driving wheels of two diameters, 190cm (75in) and 200cm (79in), were supplied.

After their appearance in 1945, the S1 Niagaras were employed on the New York-Chicago run, regularly working through the 930 miles from Harmon, where they took over from the electric locomotives that brought the trains out of Grand Central Station, to Chicago. Detailed studies of their performance, compared with that of a group of diesels, were carried out, and it was found that the six Niagaras attained an availability rate of over 69%. This amounted to a yearly average mileage of 418,340km (260,000 miles), while the equi-valent figure for the diesels, which cost more than twice as much, was 530,970km (330,000 miles).

Unfortunately, the carbon-silicone steel used for the boiler shells as a weight-saving measure began to develop cracks; faced with the cost of providing new boilers, the management inevitably turned to diesels for their subsequent motive power requirements. Within a few years every other railroad followed suit, though there were attempts to prolong the use of steam.

The principal advantage of the eight-coupled layout was to concentrate weight on the driving wheels, and as a result improve adhesion. An indication of the popularity of the type in the early years of the twentieth century was the government's orders, totalling 680, for locomotives of the 2-8-0 wheel arrangement for military service in France during the First World War. By early 1918 no fewer than 30 were being completed every day, though by then bigger types were being adopted for regular use.

Since freight locomotives were not called on to match the high speeds required in passenger service, two-wheel leading trucks were normally used, even though the Pennsylvania

Railroad, for example, produced the first of a long series of 4-8-2s for fast freight duties in 1918. The culmination of the series was the M1a class of 1930, which weighed 347 tonnes (342 tons), including the tender, and produced a tractive effort of 29,280kg (64,550lb).

The more common freight equivalent of the Pacific passenger engine was the 2-8-2, or Mikado, and while the 9,500 or so engines built amounted to less than half the total of nearly 22,000 2-8-0s, no other type came close in terms of numbers. The Santa Fe went one better in 1903 with the production of the first 2-10-2, which used the trailing truck to give greater flexibility on the Santa Fe's mountain divisions, with their heavy grades and sharp curves.

A natural progression from the two-wheel trailing truck was to four wheels at the back which supported a firebox of increased size, and in the mid-1920s both eight-coupled and ten-coupled freight engines appeared with this arrangement. The 2-10-4 was known in the United States as the Texas type, the first being built for the Texas and Pacific Railroad in 1925, while in Canada their use in the mountain regions of the west from 1929 led to their

being called Selkirks. Use of the 2-8-4 was pioneered by the New York Central, again in 1925, which gave rise to their common name of Berkshire, after the mountains of western Massachusetts.

Among the biggest of the non-articulated freight locomotives were those 4-10-2 and 4-12-2s built by Alco for the Union Pacific from 1926. The four-wheel pilot trucks allowed the use of three cylinders, thus maximising the power that could be obtained without resorting to articulation.

Weighing 355.6 tonnes (350 tons), the 90 4-12-2s that were built gave a tractive effort of 43,818kg (96,600lb) and were capable of working 3,861-tonne (3,800-ton) trains at average speeds of 56km/h (35mph).

The biggest steam locomotives of all, however, were the articulated type. The system of articulation used on American railroads was first developed by Anatole Mallet toward the end of the nineteenth century in France, and this involved the use of a single boiler to supply two sets of cylinders. The steam was used first by a pair of high-pressure cylinders and then fed to a low-pressure pair, but the distinguishing feature of the Mallet system as against other compound systems was

the use of two sets of driving wheels on separate chassis, the leading chassis being arranged so that it could turn and swivel and thus negotiate curves satisfactorily.

The first Mallet built in North America was delivered by Alco to the Baltimore and Ohio Railroad in 1904, and within a few years Mallets were very popular for heavy freight duties. As the number of driving wheels was increased from 12 to 16 and even 20, leading and trailing trucks were added to improve riding qualities and later to support an enlarged firebox. The most popular configuration was the 2-6-6-2, while the biggest of the Mallets were the Union Pacific's 4-8-8-4 Big Boys of 1941. The latter were the biggest steam locomotives ever

Above: *Challenger Class at Laramie in May 1983. A Big Boy locomotive is illustrated on the title page of this book*

Challenger class 4-6-6-4

Railway: Union Pacific Railroad (UP)
Date: 1942
Length overall: 37.16m (121ft 11in)
Total weight: 486,818kg (1,071,000lb)
Cylinders: four 533 × 813mm (21 × 32in)
Driving wheels: 1.753m (5ft 7in)
Axle load: 30,909kg (68,000lb)
Fuel: 25,455kg (56,000lb)
Grate area: 12.3m² (132sq ft)
Water: 94,500 litres (20,800 Imp gal/25,000 US gal)
Heating surface: 431m² (4,624sq ft)
Superheater: 162m² (1,741sq ft)

built, weighing 360 tonnes (354 tons). Although not the most powerful of all locomotives, the Big Boys were built for speed and efficiency and, like their predecessors on the Union Pacific, the 4-6-6-4 Challengers, were capable of hauling express freight trains at speeds of up to 128km/h (80mph).

The Big Boys came into their own on the Union Pacific's route through the mountains between Ogden and Cheyenne, running fruit trains between Ogden and Green River, where the Challengers took over. Both these Union Pacific types, like later Mallets on other US railroads, dispensed with the compound arrangement when the low-pressure cylinders had grown so big that they could no longer be accommodated, and the valves were no longer adequate to deal with the volume of steam.

Another notable user of Mallets was the Denver and Rio Grande Western on its difficult main lines in the Rockies, while the Southern Pacific developed a cab-forward design for its mountain section of the Sierra Nevada between California and Nevada. The use of oil for fuel enabled these 4-8-8-2s, of which 195 were built between 1928 and 1944, to run backwards, in effect, with the tender trail-

ing and the engineer therefore provided with the best possible view forward.

As well as being the biggest steam locomotives built in North America, engines of the Mallet type were also among the last. After the Second World War, when the American railroads were all turning in increasing numbers toward diesel power, the Norfolk and Western Railway, the main operation of which was the transport of coal from the mining areas of Kentucky and West Virginia, made a determined effort to improve its locomotives to the point where they could compete, in terms of operating efficiency and availability, with the new diesels.

In its own design offices and its own locomotive works at Roanoake, the Norfolk and Western produced three new models. The J class 4-8-4, first built in 1941, was designed to haul the prestige passenger services at 161km/h (100mph) and more. The A class 2-6-6-4 and Y class 2-8-8-2 articulated types, dating from 1936 and 1948 respectively, were used for freight work, the A class at speeds up to 112.6km/h (70mph) and the Y6 class developing maximum power at lower speeds. The real advance with these and the Y6b type, the ultimate in develop-

ment of the Mallet, was the rationalising of maintenance facilities to the point where less than an hour was required for the complete inspection, plus refuelling and lubrication between runs. Moreover, the Y6b enabled maintenance costs to be reduced by an impressive 37% compared with their predecessors of the Y5 class.

However, even the Norfolk and Western was forced to give way to the advance of the diesel, and although the Y6b remained in production until as late as 1952, by 1957 the N&W had placed orders for 75 diesels. Its last steam locomotive, and

Above: *an FEF-3 Class 4-8-4 of UP, first introduced in 1944*

the last for any mainline railroad in the United States, was an 0-8-0 switcher produced in 1953; but the problem of keeping a steam fleet going when everyone else had turned to diesels finally forced the N & W to end steam services in 1960, the last run being made by a Y6b on April 4.

The first all-steel Pullman

Right: *two types of sleeping accommodation available in the Pullmans of US 'Limiteds' in the mid-1930s*

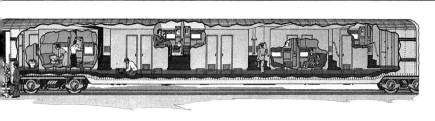

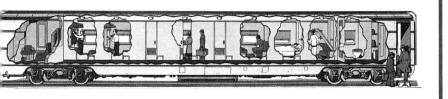

had been produced in 1907. By this time the accommodation included curtained seating sections which could be converted to incorporate berths at night, a ladies' drawing room at one end of the car, and a gentlemen's smoking compartment at the other end. Air conditioning was added in the late 1920s, and in the 1930s the 'roomette' was introduced, replacing the curtained alcoves with individual compartments that combined day seating, folding berths and toilet facilities. At first 18 roomettes were contained in each car, but by staggering the position of the floors and arranging for one bed to slide underneath the higher floor and the bed in the next compartment to fold against the wall, 24 separate roomettes were packed into one car.

Matching this improvement was the acceleration in the speed of services. The leaders in this on the Chicago run were the Pennsylvania and the New York Central, running their prestige trains, the Broadway Limited and the Twentieth Century Limited, in 18 hours, though after the war this was raised to 20 hours.

During the 1920s the last word in luxury was matched by the opulence of the catering; but as the private automobile began to make its presence felt, speed was the vital factor enabling the railroads to compete in an area where they had previously enjoyed a virtual monopoly. This trend culminated in the introduction of the streamliners in the 1930s, for the publicity value of their spectacular looks was a valuable weapon against economic depression and the growth of private transport.

The first streamliner was introduced by Union Pacific, with Pullman-built aluminium cars and a diesel engine in 1934. However, in 1935 the Milwaukee Road began operating its Hiawathas with magnificent steam locomotives. This service was initially restricted to the highly competitive trip from Chicago to Minneapolis and St Paul, but was later extended north to the shore of Lake Superior, and west to Omaha, Sioux Falls and via the Olympian Hiawatha to Spokane.

Lavish private saloons for use by the wealthiest travellers could be built to individual specifications; the only limit on what they might offer was the size of the coach and the depth of the customer's purse. The Pullman company alone built some 450 coaches for private customers before the great financial crash of 1929.

CANADA

The pioneering transcontinental railroad's opening up of the western United States in the 1870s was mirrored in the next decade by the building of the Canadian Pacific. This construction of a transcontinental railway in Canada was actually embodied in the agreement by which the former independent colony of British Columbia became part of the Canadian federation in 1871. The original stipulation was that the line should be completed within ten years, though it was another 15 years before the first trains were running between Montréal and the Pacific coast.

This was a formidable achievement, however, in view of the succession of mountain ranges in the west and the combination of swamp and rock with which the builders had to contend in their progress round the north of Lake Superior. After reaching the brink of bankruptcy during construction of the railroad and having survived a difficult period in its early years, the Canadian Pacific Railway grew to become one of the most successful rail operations in North America.

The Royal Commission

CNR Class U-4 No 6230 4-8-4, which entered service in 1936; of the 203 built, eight survive today

Preserved No 6060 of Class U1-f 4-8-2, which entered service with CNR in 1944

appointed in 1916 recommended that the Grand Trunk, Grand Trunk Pacific and Canadian Northern Railways should be brought under government control. Investigation of their finances revealed a tangled situation that took some years to sort out, but in 1918 the Canadian National Railway Company was formed to carry out the Royal Commission's recommendations.

Canadian National took over the existing publicly-owned railways and the newly-formed Canadian Northern. The Grand Trunk Pacific was added in 1920, and the parent company followed in 1923.

So as to improve the existing network, Canadian National began the construction of the lines into the Peace River area of northern Alberta, and added the Long Lac cutoff between the old Canadian northern and Grand Trunk lines, which shortened the distance between North Bay and Winnipeg by 164km (102 miles).

At about the same time, the

Canadian Pacific was busy building up a network of branches in the prairies, and during the prosperous years of the 1920s, when the Canadian National under its new management began to follow suit, there was vigorous competition between the two networks. This was brought to an end, however, by the economic depression of the 1930s, which saw dramatic falls in traffic to barely half its 1928 level. The position was so serious that consideration was even given to a merger of the two networks, but their contrasting natures made this politically impossible.

A Royal Commission was appointed at the end of 1931 and recommended a number of steps to improve co-operation between the two systems, including the pooling of passenger trains over the busiest runs between Montréal and Toronto, where competition had grown so fierce as to produce world-record scheduled runs in the early 1930s.

The gradual easing of the depression towards the end of the decade saw traffic on the increase again, and the Second

Ex-Canadian Pacific Royal Hudson Class 4-6-4 No 2860 at Vancouver, August 1990

World War brought record levels of freight movement. The massive production that was undertaken in Canada stretched the railroads to capacity, especially on the eastern lines to the Atlantic ports of Halifax and Saint John. The single track between Moncton and Halifax, which became the most important of the wartime ports, was especially busy, and in 1941 centralised train control was installed to speed up traffic on this section.

The wartime boom was followed, in Canada as elsewhere, by a severe decline in rail traffic as a result of growing competition from both road and air transport: and as on other systems, the accent had been on improving efficiency in all areas of operation.

Despite the general decline in demand, there were still areas where the rail network was being expanded in response to the need for access to undeveloped natural resources, such as the enormous iron ore deposits in the inhospitable region of eastern Québec and Labrador around Knob Lake, 563km (350 miles) north of the St Lawrence estuary.

One of the most ambitious of modern developments is that of the British Columbia Railway. The Pacific Great Eastern Railway had been chartered in 1912 to build from Squamish up through the lumber country of the Fraser valley to a connection with the Grand Trunk Railway at Prince George. Little progress was made until the provincial government took over the project at the end of the First World War, when construction was resumed. By 1921 553.5km (344 miles) had been built to Quesnel, still some way short of the planned junction at Prince George.

Early Canadian locomotives were generally of the American 4-4-0 type, and for the services between Montréal and Ottawa Canadian Pacific had produced a design of the Atlantic type 4-4-2 in 1899. These were four-cylinder compound engines, and they were able to operate some 77.3km/h (48mph) services, including intermediate stops, between the two cities.

SOUTH AMERICA

Here the railway systems share some of the characteristics of those in Africa, having been started by foreign promoters, largely British and American, using a mixture of gauges, tending to carry natural resources from inland sources to coastal ports, and to link the most important coastal cities.

The railways of Argentina were operated by predominantly British companies until nationalisation in 1949: at that point they were in need of large scale modernisation, and the position was not made easier by the existence of three separate gauges, the broad gauge 167.6cm (5ft 6in), the standard gauge and metre gauge, with additional lines of narrow gauge.

An example of the narrow gauge operations is provided by the 402.5km (250 mile) branch line from Ingeniero Jacobacci to Esquel. Built to the 76.2cm (2ft 6in) gauge and operated by steam, this line has many of the characteristics of the rural railway, with slow, mixed trains serving the needs of a sparsely populated area.

A contrast with the Argentine operation is offered by the line through the Bolivian Andes from Rio Mulato to Potosi. At its highest point, this line reaches some 4,787m (15,705ft) at Condor, barely 30.5m (100ft) below the highest railway in the world, at La Cima in Peru. The style of service is similar, however: a weekly mixed freight and passenger train hauled by a 2-8-2 locomotive on a metre-gauge track.

It is fitting to end in Peru, for it was here that Richard Trevithick, the man who started it all, turned up in 1816 on his gold mining expedition. He produced a railway over the 15.3km (9.5 miles) between Lima and the port of Callão, but the wars of independence of the early nineteenth century prevented the realisation of this scheme until 1851, by which time Trevithick had returned to England and died.

The line from Lima to Callão eventually formed part of the Central Railway of Peru, which includes the high point of La Cima. The other Peruvian railway, also standard gauge, is the Southern. Motive power on this line included oil-burning Baldwin 4-6-0s providing a daily passenger service.

Of course, to characterise all South American railways as quaint rural and mountain survivals from another age would be wrong.

INDIA AND THE PACIFIC

Shortly after Independence was achieved in 1947, and with it Partition and the separation of the railway system into Indian and also Pakistani administrations, the introduction of new standard classes of locomotives was begun. The Pacific type had been selected by the Locomotive Standard Committee in the 1920s, as permitting large fireboxes and grates suitable for low grades of coal, and the light, intermediate and heavy

WP Class No 7697 with a passenger train in December 1979

designs of classes XA, XB and XC were produced for the broad-gauge lines. Corresponding YB Pacifics and ZB 2-6-2s were evolved for the metre and narrow-gauge lines, while for freight work XD and even bigger XE 2-8-2s for the broad gauge and smaller YD and ZE 2-8-2s for others completed the range.

For all the achievements of the builders of the 64,000km (40,000 mile) Indian railway network, and of the administrators in running a transport system for so many people, the most famous of all India's railways is a little 61cm (2ft) gauge line that twists its way from

Siliguri up into the foothills of the Himalayas and the old hill station of Darjeeling.

This line was begun in 1879, and in reaching its destination at a height of 2,255.5m (7,400ft) the line goes through five zig-zags and four spirals, not in tunnels but on the open hill side. Consequently, the Hima-layan scenery provides more than adequate compensation for the seven hours that are spent in completing the 88.6km (55 mile) climb.

The locomotives used on the Darjeeling line are of an 0-4-0T saddle tank design first built in 1879, five years after the open-ing of the railway. The newest date from 1927, and of the total of 30 that were procured at intervals most are still opera-tional.

Until 1937, the Indian railway system extended into Burma, which before that date was administered as a province of the Indian Empire, but the metre-gauge Burma Railway never made any connections

Above: *HP Class No 24444 at Kanpur Shed, November 1979*

Left: *a Class YP 4-6-2 still in excellent running condition; production of the class began in 1949 and lasted through 871 units, until 1970*

with the railways of its eastern neighbour, Thailand. These were standard gauge when construction began in the 1890s, but were converted after the First World War to conform with the metre gauge adopted by the Southern Railway when the latter was built south to a connection with the Malayan state system.

The various lines of the Thai railways radiate out from Bangkok, reaching the borders of Laos and Cambodia, and the locomotives used were all imported from various foreign builders, including Britain, the United States and Japan. Since the early 1960s, when diesels took over passenger services, steam has been gradually eliminated, but while it was used the two most obvious characteristics of the locomotives were their clean appearance and the use of wood for fuel.

The normal object of colonial administrations in building railways was as a method of either extending control of the territory or of exploiting its natural resources. In the latter case, railways were not necessarily public carriers: one of the most widespread applications of narrow gauge steam railways was in sugar plantations, where a lightly-laid track would enable a small locomotive to collect wagons loaded with the cane, often collected on temporary feeder lines by animal traction.

An example of this practice, combined with a public railway, occurred on the island of Fiji. Grants made to the Colonial Sugar Corporation to enable it to cultivate plantations of sugar cane stipulated that the company should work a free passenger railway, and little 4-4-0 locomotives, built by the British company of Hudswell-Clarke and of a type commonly used for light industrial and agricultural work, operated the passenger service on a 61cm (2ft) gauge track. These were later to be replaced by diesel engines.

At the other end of the scale of steam railway operation is the Chinese state system. In the nineteenth century, the Imperial government resisted railways, as they had resisted the other innovations of the western powers which attempted to colonise parts of the country. Railways were built more or less as military superiority allowed, and the years of anti-western uprisings, civil war, Japanese occupation and more civil war that occupied most of the first half of the twentieth century meant that railway construction did not

Above: *Chinese RM Class No 1123 at Shenyang North*

Below: *Chinese JF Class No 4065, Changchun East Junction, 1989*

begin in earnest until the establishment of the communist government in 1949.

In the Pacific, steam railways in Australia and New Zealand are now in the hands of the preservation organisations, diesel and electric traction now having taken over main-line operations.

The Australian railways were slow to develop in the early stages. A sparse population, concentrated in widely dispersed centres, and separate colonial administrations in six different regions, led to initial building of more or less local ines. More seriously, an early greement between Victoria, South Australia and New South Vales to adopt a gauge of 160cm 5ft 3in) was broken by New South Wales, which changed to tandard gauge: the other two tates, having already ordered road-gauge locomotives, went head with the agreed measure, so that when the first railways vere opened in the 1850s there vere two different gauges in use.

The situation became more complicated during the 1860s and 1870s, when the other states began building their first railways. Tasmania followed both Victoria and South Australia in using 160cm (5ft 3in) gauge, but Queensland and Western Australia went for economy of construction with yet a third gauge, this time of 106.7cm (3ft 6in), which was later applied to the Tasmanian system and to some lines built in South Australia.

The consequence of all this variety in the gauges was that Victoria and South Australia

Above: *1944-built Australian Class 520 4-8-4*

Below: *fully restored at ARHS Museum, Mile End, and photographed in September 1967, Class 500 No 504 of SAR*

were the only two states with a common border and the same gauge of railway. Moreover, full advantage was taken of the narrow gauge's opportunity for light track, relatively sharp grades and tight curves, so that subsequent development was restricted by the track within states as well as by the gauge changes between them. The immense variety of locomotives that appeared as imported models were supplemented by the various states' own production, and well represented by the numerous museums and preservation societies.

The same is true of New Zealand, where agreement over gauges hindered the early building of railways. New Zealand ultimately standardised on a gauge of 106.7cm (3ft 6in), and all lines were of this gauge by the end of the 1870s.

In 1906 one of the most successful of all New Zealand's own steam locomotive designs appeared, in the shape of the A class Pacific, a four-cylinder compound on the de Glehn system. A total of 57 were built, and after a long career on the express services, some were still at work on coal trains when steam was finally superseded by diesel power on the west coast lines in 1969.

When further examples were

Six Class Kb locomotives were built with boosters, which provided an extra 3,640kg (8,000lb) of tractive effort; Kb 967 is pictured in 1967 on a fan trip from Timaru to Christchurch

required in 1914, the outbreak of the First World War mean British builders were unable to accept any orders, and a serie of ten 4-6-2s, designated the A class, were obtained from Baldwins in the United States. A more significant type, however was the Ab class, of the next year, that used superheating to dispense with the A class compound operation, and featured the novel Vanderbilt type of tender, which incorporated a cylindrical water tank. A total of 141 were built, mostly in New Zealand, with further examples supplied by the North British Locomotive Company.

Later New Zealand types included the K class 4-8-4 designed to be the most powerful locomotive possible, given the rather restricted loading gauge on the New Zealand lines The 30 original Ks were supplemented by the improved Ka class, and by the Kb type which added a booster unit for use on the most heavily graded sections on the South Island.

AFRICA

The geographical and political difficulties that have attended the building of railways in Africa have prevented the evolution of anything like a comprehensive network. Generally railways have been built for specific purposes, usually to enable the products of inland mines to be carried to the coasts, and to minimise the cost and difficulty of doing so they have been built to metre or 106.7cm (3ft 6in) gauges.

At one stage the colonist Cecil Rhodes had ambitions to build a railway from the Cape of Good Hope to Cairo, uniting the various British colonies and also consolidating the British administration from Egypt to South Africa. This grandiose scheme ignored both the rivalry between the various colonial powers and sheer scale of the physical barriers.

The latter were encountered in full measure by the builders of the Uganda Railway, begun from Mombasa in 1896, and which was forced to climb a series of escarpments, culminating in the 2,538m (8,327ft) Mau summit, before reaching its goal of Lake Victoria. Although built to the 106.7cm (3ft 6in) gauge, the Uganda Railway was ultimately con-

verted to metre gauge and formed the basis for the East African Railway, connecting Uganda and the Kenyan capital of Nairobi with the port of Mombasa.

Articulation was an early strategy employed in order to obtain sufficient power for working the heavy trains made necessary by the predominantly single-track and narrow gauge lines with restricted loading gauges, and the Mallet type that was developed so successfully in North America was the first to be used of the modern types of articulated locomotive. The Mallet system, however, which mounts a large boiler on two powered bogies, while per-

Top: *Class 16E locomotive No 858, one of just five high-speed 4-6-2s of 1935, built for the Cape Town to Johannesburg 1,530km (956-mile) journey, which was scheduled in 30 hours*

Centre: *Class 25 4-8-4s were condensing locomotives, designed to overcome the water shortages in the Karoo Desert*

Bottom: *Class 15A of Rhodesian Railways (Zimbabwe) at Deka Sidings, with a goods train from Victoria Falls to Thomson Junction*

mitting curves to be negotiated readily, demands a long and cumbersome boiler and, especially in its original compound form, resulted in locomotives of great complexity.

Early in the twentieth century, an Australian engineer, Herbert Garratt, developed a new system of articulation, which involved mounting the water tank and fuel bunker on separate engine units fore and aft of the boiler, which is carried between the two. As well as allowing the locomotive to pivot at two points, the Garratt system has a number of other advantages. A high adhesion weight is spread over a long wheelbase, a large diameter of boiler can be used, and the firebox grate can be deep and wide, since there are no wheels and axles underneath to limit its size.

The Garratts were developed by the British firm of Beyer Peacock, and these Beyer-Garratt locomotives proved ideal for African conditions immediately it was introduced in South Africa shortly after the First World War.

The decisive year for Beyer-Garratt was 1921. At first its sponsors believed the idea's potential was best realised by building the articulateds as compounds, but in 1921 a simple

expansion 2-6-0 + 0-6-2 supplied to the 106.7cm (3ft 6in) gauge South African Railways dispelled that theory. Evaluated against a local Mallet, it proved unmistakably superior both as a performer and in terms of fuel consumption. This set the scene for subsequent development of the narrow-gauge and simple-expansion Beyer-Garratt as haulier that was the equal of most European heavy freight engines in tractive effort.

On East Railways, the biggest Garratts were introduced in 1955 as the 59 class. These were to be the most powerful metre-gauge locomotives to be built for any railway, and were capable of handling 1,220 tonne (1,200 ton) freight trains to climb from Mombasa to Nairobi. The 59 class has the wheel arrangement 4-8-2 + 2-8-4; earlier classes had pioneered the 4-8-4 + 4-8-4 arrangement for use on lighter sections of track.

The former Rhodesian Railways was also a great user of Garratts. More amenable terrain allowed generally higher speeds to be reached with passenger services, and some of the fastest Garratt types were used, though their introduction also allowed an enormous increase in the volume of freight handled.

The Rhodesian railways were originally an extension of the Cape Province system, and so were built to the Cape gauge of 106.7cm (3ft 6in). Although the Beyer-Garratt first proved its ability on South African Railways and it has seen extensive use there since the 1920s, most locomotives used were of more conventional design.

To compensate for the sloth of its passenger trains, a notable line in luxury trains was developed in South Africa. The famous Blue Train between Cape Town and Johannesburg had originated in the Union Limited, established in 1903 to connect with the arrival of the Union Castle mail ship from England.

A South African Railways Class 59 Beyer-Garrett shifts heavy freight

Class 59 4-8-2 + 2-8-4

Railway: East African Railways (EAR)
Date: 1955
Length overall: 31.737m (104ft 1.5in)
Total weight: 256,364kg (564,000lb)
Cylinders: four 521 × 711mm (20.5 × 28in)
Driving wheels: 1.372m (4ft 6in)
Axle load: 21,364kg (47,000lb)
Fuel: 12,267 litres (2,700 Imp gal/3,250 US gal) oil
Grate area: 6.7m² (72sq ft)
Water: 39,044 litres (8,600 Imp gal/10,400 US gal)

Above: *LNER V2 Class No 4771 Green Arrow has been preserved in the National Railway Museum, York*

Left: *40 Schools Class 4-4-0 locomotives were built for Southern Region between 1930 and 1935*

Below: *the Duchess Class was the most powerful locomotive to run in the UK*

Above: *800 Class 4-6-0s were the last steam locomotives to be built in Ireland*

Left: *Netherlands State Railway Class 3700 No 3724 in 1956*

Below: *Romanian State Railways preserved Class 142*

Above right: *GS 4 No 4999 meets 2472 at Sacramento in 1991*

Below right: *the ultimate Soviet steam locomotive was the P36 Class*

0-4-0

2-2-2

0-6-0

4-4-0

2-4-0

4-6-0

0-6-2

4-6-2

4-4-2

2-10-0

2-8-4

WHEEL NOTATION

Steam locomotives are described by a three-figure combination which refers to the number of wheels, usually made up of driving wheels (shown *left* as black open circles) and bogie or trailing wheels (shown in blue). The first figure denotes the number of bogie wheels at the front, the second gives the number of driving wheels, and the third the number of trailing wheels. If the locomotive is a tank engine, a 'T' is added after the third figure. If the locomotive is articulated with a fourth figure added, the second and third figures refer to the driving wheels.

Below: *King Class No 6002. The 30 four-cylinder King Class 4-6-0s replaced the less powerful Castles, which had in turn replaced the Star Class locomotives, with each basically being a stretched version of its predecessor. Derived from the de Glehn arrangement, with the outside cylinders driving the coupled axle, and the inside pair driving the leading axle, both sets of cylinders were horizontal, with each adjacent pair being diametrically opposed.*

The working parts of a King Class 4-6-0 locomotive, first built in 1927 for the Great Western Railway

Length overall: 20.777m (68ft 2in)
Total weight: 138,181kg (304,000lb)
Cylinders: four 413 × 711mm (16.25 × 28in)
Driving wheels: 1.981m (6ft 6in)

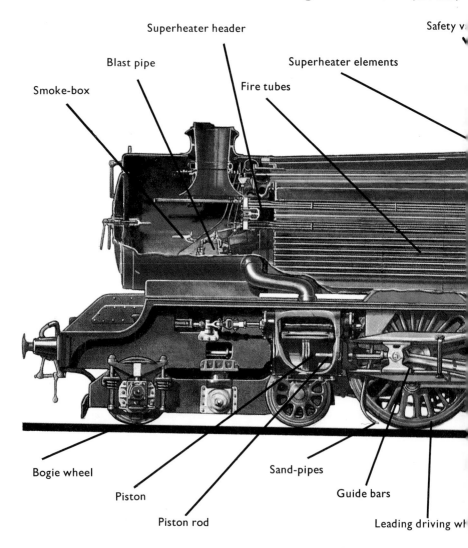

Superheater header

Blast pipe

Smoke-box

Safety v

Superheater elements

Fire tubes

Bogie wheel

Piston

Piston rod

Sand-pipes

Guide bars

Leading driving wl

Axle load: 22.954kg (50,500lb)
Fuel: 6,136kg (13,500lb)
Grate area: 3.19m² (343sq ft)
Water: 18,160 litres (4,000 Imp gal/4,800 US gal)
Heating surface: 204m² (2,201sq ft)

Superheater: 29m² (313sq ft)
Steam pressure: 17.6kg/cm² (250psi)
Adhesive weight: 68,636kg (151,000lb)
Tractive effort: 18,285kg (40,300lb)

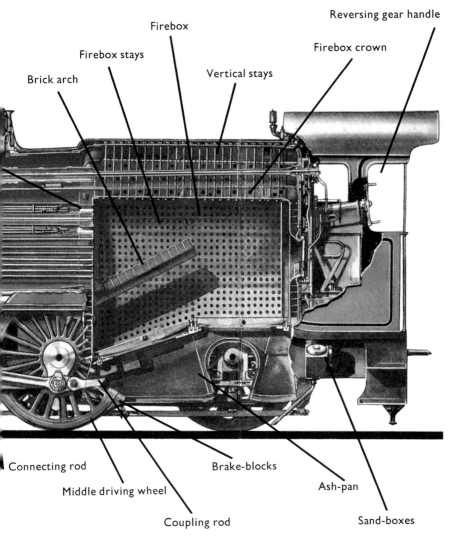

Reversing gear handle

Firebox

Firebox crown

Firebox stays

Vertical stays

Brick arch

Connecting rod

Brake-blocks

Middle driving wheel

Ash-pan

Coupling rod

Sand-boxes

INDEX

A Class (New Zealand) 82
Ab Class (New Zealand) 82
Allegheny Corporation 56
Association of American
    Railroads (AAR) 58
American Locomotive
    Company (Alco) 62, 64, 67, 68
Atchison, Topeka and Santa
    Fe 67
Atlantic Class (Great
    Britain) **30**
Austrian Federal Railway
    (ÖBB) 6
Austro-Hungarian Empire 6
Austrian State Railway 6
Austrian Südbahn 5

Baker valve gear 62
Baldwin 64, 76, 82
Baltimore and Ohio Railroad
    (B & O) 55, **56**, 68
Battle of Britain Class (Great
    Britain) 40
Belgian National Railways 7
Belpaire firebox 33
Beyer-Garratt 85, 86
Beyer Peacock 85
Big Boy **1**, 68, 69
Black Five 36
Blue Train 86
Borsig 28
Boston and Maine 56
British Columbian Railway
    75
British Railways (BR) 43
Broadway Limited 72
Bulleid, Oliver 40
Burma Railway 78

Caerphilly Castle 33
Caffiers Bank 15
Calais-Mediterranean 50
Caledonian Railway 31, 32, 34
Canadian National Railways
    (CNR) 73
Canadian Northern Railways
    74
Canadian Pacific Railroad 73,
    74
Cardean 31
Cardean Class (Great
    Britain) 31
Castle Class (Great Britain)
    33, **34**, 35, 38
Central Railway of Peru 76
Challenger Class (USA) **68**, 69
Chapelon, André 12, 13, 14, 15,
    18, 19
Cheltenham Flyer 33
Chicago Minneapolis and St
    Paul 72
Churchwood, George 12, 32,
    33, 35, 38

City Class (Great Britain) **31**,
    32
City of Truro 32
Class A (USA) 64, 69
    A3 (Great Britain) 38, **39**
    A3/5 (Switzerland) **49**
    A4 (Great Britain) 11, **37**, 38,
        39, 40
    BR9 (Great Britain) 45
    E6 (USA) 59
    F3 (USA) 64
    F4 (USA) 64
    F5 (USA) 64
    F6 (USA) 64
    F7 (USA) 64
    F2001 (Spain) 47
    GS-2 (USA) 65
    GS-4 (USA) **65**
    HP (India) **78**
    K5 (USA) 62
    L3 (USA) 62
    M1a (USA) 67
    P8 (Prussia) **23**
    S1 (USA) 64, 66
    S160 (Germany) 26
    U-4 (Canada) 73
    XA (India) 77
    XB (India) 77
    XC (India) 77
    XD (India) 77
    XE (India) 77
    YB (India) 77
    YD (India) 77
    YP (India) **78**
    ZB 77
    ZE 77
01 (Germany) 24, **25**, 27, **29**
02 (Germany) 24
03 (Germany) 27, 29
05 (Germany) 25, 28
06 (Germany) 29
9 (Great Britain) **43**
10 (France) 20
12 (Belgium) 7
15a (Zimbabwe) **84**
16E (South Africa) 84
25 (South Africa) 84
42 (Germany) 26
44 (Germany) **26**
50 (Germany) 26
52 (Germany) 26
59 (South Africa) 85, **86**
141 P (France) 18
141 R (France) **16/17**, 18, 19,
    20
210 (Austria) **5**
221 A (France) 18
230 D (France) 10
231 C (France) **13**
232 R (France) 20
232 S (France) 20
232 U (France) **20**
240 P (France) 18
241 C (France) **15**
241 P (France) 20
242 (Spain) **47**
310 (Austria) 4

498.1 (Czechoslovakia) **8**
500 (Australia) **81**
520 (Australia) **81**
640 (Italy) **44**
685 (Italy) **46**
743 (Italy) 45
4500 (France) **10**
Collin 11
Cornish Riviera Express 32
Coronation Scot 38, 40
Crosti, Piero 45
Crova, Carlo 45

Dalziel, Lord Davidson 51, 52
de Bousquet 9, 10, 11
de Glehn compounding 9, 10,
    82
Denver and Rio Grande
    Western 69
Deutsche Bundesbahn (DB)
    20, 27, 29
Deutsche Reichsbahn (DR)
    27, 28, 29

East African Railway (EAR)
    84, 86
Eastern Region 42
East Railways 85
Edelweiss Pullman 54
Emergency Transportation
    Act (1940) 58
Engerth 48
Est Railway 12
État Railway 11
Euston 31
Evening Star 43

FEF-3 Class (USA) 70
First World War 5, 6, 8, 9, 10,
    21, 23, 33, 45, 56, 66, 75, 79, 82,
    85
Flèche d'or 51, **53**
Franco, Attilo 45
French Railways (SNCF) 10,
    15, 18, 19, 20
Furka-Oberalp Railway 48

Gare de Lyons 50, 51
Gare du Nord 11, 51
Garrett, Herbert 85
General Steam Navigation **41**
Genf 48
Gölsdorf, Karl 4, 5
Gotthard Tunnel 48
Gould 55
Grand Central Station 66
Grand Trunk Pacific 74
Grand Trunk Railway 74, 75
Great Bear 36
Great Eastern 34
Great Northern Railway
    (GNR) 30, 34, 38
Great Western Railway
    (GWR) 12, 31, 32, 34, 35, 36, 42
Gresley, Nigel 38, 40

Harriman, Ed 55

20TH CENTURY STEAM LOCOMOTIVES HANDBOOK

Hiawatha 64, 72
Hill, Jim 55
Hudswell-Clarke 79

Imperial and Royal Austrian
 State Railways (KKStB's) 4
Interstate Commerce
 Commission (ICC) 55, 58, 59
Italian State Railways (FS)
 45, 46

J Class (USA) 69
JF Class (China) **80**
J1 Hudson (USA) 62, **63**

Ka Class (New Zealand) 82
Kb Class (New Zealand) 82, **83**
King Arthur Class (Great
 Britain) 35
King Class (Great Britain) **91**,
 92/3
King's Cross 11, 38
Krupps 20
Kylchap double exhausts 8, 13

Lady Superior 32
Lancashire and Yorkshire
 Railway (L & Y R) 30
Lehigh Valley Railroad 56
Locomotive Standard
 Committee 77
London Midland and Scottish
 (LMS) 27, 34, 36, 38, 42
London Midland Region 42
London and North Eastern
 Railway (LNER) 11, 18, 34,
 37, 38, 40
London and North Western 34
London and South Western
 34, 35
London Passenger Transport
 Board 40
Lord Nelson Class (Great
 Britain) 35, **36**

Maffei Company 24
Mallard 20
Mallet, Anatole 67
Marshall Aid 19
McIntosh, J F 31
Merchant Navy Class (Great
 Britain) 40, **41**
Midland Railways 30, 34
Milwaukee Road 64, 72
Morgan, Pierpont 55
Mussolini 45, 46

National Transportation
 Committee (NTC) 58
New York Central (NYC) 62,
 63, 66, 67, 72
Niagara Class 62, **63**, 66
Nickel Plate line 56
Nord Express 9
 Railway 9, 10, 11, 20
Norfolk & Western Railway
 (N & W) 56, 69, 70

Norte Railway 47
North British Locomotive
 Company 11, 82
North Eastern Railway
 (NER) 30, 34, 38
North Eastern Region 42

Office of Defense
 Transportation 59
Oiseau Bleu 9

Pacific Great Eastern
 Railway 75
Paddington 32, 33, 43
Papyrus 38
Paris-Lyons-Méditerranée
 (PLM) 10, 11, 12, 13, 18, 20, 50
Paris-Mediterranean 50
Paris-Orléans Railway **10**, 11,
 14, 15
Pennsylvania Railroad 55, 56,
 59, 62, 66, 72
Philadelphia and Reading
 Railroad 59
Princess Class (Great
 Britain) 38
Pullman 9, 51, 52, 53, **71**, 72

Railway Executive
 Committee 40, 42
Railways Act (1921) 36
Raven, Sir Vincent 38
Reichsbahn Gesellschaft 21,
 22, 24, 25, 26, 54
Rheingold 9
Rhodes, Cecil 83
Rhodesian Railways
 (Zimbabwe) **84**, 85, 86
Riddles 27
RM Class (China) **80**
Roosevelt, President
 Theodore D 58
Royal Hudson Class (Canada)
 75
Royal Prussian Union
 Railway (KPEV) 23
Royal Scot 38

St Pancras 30
Saint Class (Great Britain)
 32, **33**
Schmidt, Wilhelm 59
Scottish Region 42
Second World War 6, 19, 25,40,
 54, 69
Semmering Pass 5, 48
Shap Summit 31
Silver Jubilee **37**, 38, 40
Silver Link 38
South African Railways 85, 86
South Australia Railway 81
Southern Region 42, 53
Southern Railway (India) 79
Southern Railway (SR)
 (Great Britain) 34, 35
Spanish Civil War 47
Spanish National Railways

(RENFE) 47
Stanier, William 27, 36
Star Class (Great Britain) 33
Stephenson, Robert 48
Sud Express 53
Sunshine Express 54
Survilliers Bank 15
Swiss Federal Railways
 (SBB) 49

Texas and Pacific Railroad 67
Third Reich 26, 27, 28
Train, Blue 51
Train de luxe 50, **51**
Trans-Manchurian Express 52
Trans-Siberian Express 52
Treaty of Versailles 6, 21
Trevithick, Richard 76
Twentieth Century Limited
 62, **63**, 72

Uganda Railway 83
Ul-f Class (Canada) 74
Union Limited 86
Union Pacific 67, 68, 69, 70, 72
US Railroad Administration
 56

Vanderbilt 55, 82
Van Swerigen 56, 57, 58
Vauclain compound system
 64

Wabash 56
Wagon-Lits 50, **52**
Wagner, R P 24, 25, 27, 28
Walschaert's valve gear 14,
 36, 62
West Country Class (Great
 Britain) 40
Western Region 42
William Dean 32
Wootten, John 59
WP Class (India) **77**

Y Class (USA) 69
Y5 Class (USA) 70
Y6 Class (USA) 69
Y6b Class (USA) 69, 70

95

The Red Dragon train, hauled by Class 8 prototype the **Duke of Gloucester,** *which was designed as an express passenger locomotive. Testing proved satisfactory, but it was too late for further steam traction development in Great Britain, and the* **Duke of Gloucester** *was scrapped*

ACKNOWLEDGMENTS

Photographs are reproduced by courtesy of Colour-Rail, Chesham, with additional photographs supplied by TRH Pictures, London, and from the Superlaunch library.

Additional artworks were supplied by Andrew Wright, London